The *Ministry* of *Visitation*

JOHN T. SISEMORE

CONVENTION PRESS
Nashville, Tennessee

Church Study Course for Teaching and Training
This work is number 1708 in Category 17, section A
Library of Congress Catalog Card Number: 54:2969

Printed in the United States of America
95. F 61 R.R.D.

ABOUT THE AUTHOR

JOHN T. SISEMORE was born near Lawton, Oklahoma, April 9, 1913. Inasmuch as his father was a Baptist preacher he spent most of his earlier years in parsonages in Oklahoma and Texas. Mr. Sisemore graduated from the Amarillo High School in 1930, and from the Moody Bible Institute in 1934. He did additional work at the Chicago Music College, Chicago Conservatory, Multnomah College, and Southern Baptist Theological Seminary. In 1934 he married Margaret Dornhoefer, the daughter of a preacher.

For a number of years Mr. Sisemore served in churches as education and music director, first, for the Buchanan Street Baptist Church, Amarillo, Texas (1934–1944), and then for the Hillcrest Baptist Church, Dallas, Texas (1944–1950). During the nine and a half years at Buchanan Street, every resident church member was enrolled in Sunday school. While in Texas he served as associational Sunday school superintendent for several years, was an officer in the Southwestern Religious Education Association, and was approved Adult worker for Texas under Dr. G. S. Hopkins.

From 1950 to 1957 Mr. Sisemore was director of the Department of Religious Education for the Oregon-Washington Baptist Convention, with headquarters at Portland, Oregon. Since April 15, 1957 he has served as superintendent of Adult work for the Sunday School Department, Baptist Sunday School Board.

Mr. Sisemore is the author of three other books *Program Planning and Presentation* (English and Spanish editions) *Building Better Programs in the Training Union,* and *The Sunday School Ministry to Adults.*

A Visit

One day I rang a doorbell
   In a casual sort of way,
'Twas not a formal visit
   And there wasn't much to say.

I don't remember what I said—
   It matters not I guess—
I found a heart in hunger;
   A soul in deep distress.

He said I came from Heaven,
   And I often wondered why;
He said I came to see him
   When no other help was nigh.

It meant so little to me
   To knock at a stranger's door,
But it meant Heaven to him
   And God's peace forevermore.

—E. J. Morgan

Pure religion and undefiled before God and the Father is this, To visit . . . James 1:27

Contents

CHURCH STUDY COURSE FOR TEACHING AND TRAINING

THE CHURCH STUDY COURSE FOR TEACHING AND TRAINING began October 1, 1959. It is a merger of three courses previously promoted by the Sunday School Board—the Sunday School Training Course, the Graded Training Union Study Course, and the Church Music Training Course.

The course is fully graded. The system of awards provides a series of five diplomas of twenty books each for Adults or Young People, one diploma of ten books for Young People, two diplomas of five books each for Intermediates, and two diplomas of five books each for Juniors. Book awards earned previously in the Sunday School Training Course, the Graded Training Union Study Course, and the Church Music Training Course may be transferred to the new course.

The course is comprehensive, with books grouped into nineteen categories. The purpose of the course is to (1) help Christians to grow in knowledge and conviction; (2) help them to grow toward maturity in Christian character and competence for service; (3) encourage them to participate worthily as workers in their churches; and (4) develop leaders for all phases of church life and work.

The Church Study Course for Teaching and Training is promoted by the Baptist Sunday School Board, 127 Ninth Avenue, North, Nashville, Tennessee, through its Sunday School, Training Union, Church Music, and Church Administration departments, and by these same departments in the states affiliated with the Southern Baptist Convention. A complete description of the course and the system of awards may be found in the *Church Study Course for Teaching and Training* catalog, which may be obtained without charge from any one of these departments.

A record of all awards earned should be maintained in each church. A person should be designated by the church to keep the files. Forms for such records may be ordered from any Baptist Book Store.

REQUIREMENTS FOR CREDIT IN CLASS
OR HOME STUDY

IF credit is desired for the study of this book in a class or by home study, the following requirements must be met:

I. IN CLASSWORK

1. The class must meet a minimum of seven and one-half clock hours. The required time does not include assembly periods. Ten class periods of forty-five minutes each are recommended. (If laboratory or clinical work is desired in specialized or technical courses, this requirement may be met by six clock hours of classwork and three clock hours of supervised laboratory or clinical work.)

2. A class member who attends all class sessions and completes the reading of the book within a week following the last class session will not be required to do any written work.

3. A class member who is absent from one or more sessions must answer the questions (pp. 114–116) on all chapters he misses. In such a case, he must turn in his paper within a week, and he must certify that he has read the book.

4. The teacher should request an award for himself. A person who teaches a book in section B, C, or D of any category or conducts an approved unit of instruction for Nursery, Beginner, or Primary children will be granted an award in category 11, Special Studies, which will count as an elective on his own diploma. He should specify in his request the name of the book taught, or the unit conducted for Nursery, Beginner, or Primary children.

5. The teacher should complete the "Request for Book Awards—Class Study" (Form 150) and forward it within two weeks after the completion of the class to the Church Study Course Awards Office, 127 Ninth Avenue, North, Nashville 3, Tennessee.

II. IN HOME STUDY

1. A person who does not attend any class session may receive credit by answering all questions for written work as indicated in the book (pp. 114–116). When a person turns in his paper on home study, he must certify that he has read the book.

2. Students may find profit in studying the text together, but individual papers are required. Carbon copies or duplicates in any form cannot be accepted.

3. Home study work papers may be graded by the pastor or a person designated by him, or they may be sent to the Church Study Course Awards Office for grading. The form entitled "Request for Book Awards— Home Study" (Form 151) must be used in requesting awards. It should be mailed to Church Study Course Awards Office, 127 Ninth Avenue, North, Nashville 3, Tennessee.

III. CREDIT FOR THIS BOOK

This book is No. 1708 in category 17, section A.

Foreword

THE ministry of visitation seems almost to have been overlooked by Christian authors. The apparent lack of a comprehensive treatment of this subject, plus the realization that church workers desperately need training in the art of visitation, has prompted this contribution.

The ideas presented here are the outgrowth of twenty years of experience in the field of religious education as a Sunday school teacher, Sunday school superintendent, minister of education, and state Sunday school secretary. The churches which the author has served have been willing to experiment so that the ideas presented here could be tested for practicability.

Ineffable gratitude is acknowledged to these churches, their workers, and personal friends who have rendered valuable assistance. No claim of originality is made since this material was gleaned from many sources. All quotations are properly acknowledged when the source is known. Any deviations will be gladly corrected when possible.

This book was prepared and is sent forth with the prayer that it might be helpful to those faithful Christians who take seriously the scriptural injunction to ....

"GO ... SEEK ... FIND"

CHAPTER 1

I. VISITATION WAS ESTABLISHED BY THE HEAVENLY FATHER

    1. It Began in the Garden of Eden

    2. It Served as a Contact Between God and His People

    3. It Was Culminated at Calvary

II. VISITATION WAS THE METHOD OF THE LORD JESUS

    1. He Visited in the Homes of the People

    2. He Sent His Disciples into the Homes of the People

    3. He Made Wayside Visits

    4. He Visited Specific Individuals

    5. He Visited Family Groups

    6. He Visited the Crowded Places

III. VISITATION WAS PRACTICED BY THE EARLY CHRISTIANS

    1. Peter Believed in Visitation

    2. John Preferred Visitation

    3. Paul Was a Consistent Visitor

IV. VISITATION WAS THE PROGRAM OF THE NEW TESTAMENT CHURCHES

    1. The Church at Jerusalem Had a Visitation Program

    2. The Church at Antioch Was Established as a Result of Visitation

    3. The Church at Philippi Was a Monument to the Effectiveness of Visitation

    4. The Churches at Rome were Zealous in Visitation

V. VISITATION WAS A FACTOR IN THE REMARKABLE SPREAD OF CHRISTIANITY

    1. Visitation Won Half of the World's Population in a Short Time

    2. Visitation Built Enormous Church Memberships

Realizing the Importance of Visitation

IT was in Galilee on a mountain "where Jesus had appointed them." Forty days had passed and the post-resurrection ministry of Jesus had come to a close. Jesus had met the disciples for their last appointment. This was a solemn conference, the details of which are unknown. It was unquestionably concerned with continuing the work Jesus had begun.

Jesus realized that the disciples needed encouragement and instruction for carrying on the work. The future of the church must be left in their hands. One of the disciples must have asked the Lord how they were to proceed, and in so doing he prompted those momentous words of Jesus: "Go ye therefore, and teach all nations, baptizing them in the name of the Father, and of the Son, and of the Holy Ghost: teaching them to observe all things whatsoever I have commanded you: and, lo, I am with you alway, even unto the end of the world" (Matt. 28:19-20).

With this statement Jesus not only gave them the method and plan for carrying on the work, but he also assured them of his continuing presence and power.

The plan of work which Jesus outlined was simple enough. Mark records it in an abbreviated form: "Go ye into all the world, and preach the gospel to every creature" (Mark 16:15). This divine directive can be reduced to only two small words of four letters, "Go ye." This was the Lord's plan for continuing his ministry among men. The plan was not only simple; it was highly practical. It was nothing more than reaching the nearest person, winning him to Christ, and then teaching him to do the same for others. Thus, through an ever-widening circle, the whole world could learn of the grace of God. With the giving of this plan, the ministry of visitation burst into full bloom.

Contrary to the opinion of some, the Lord's command was not primarily a command to foreign mission effort. To be sure, it included this witness to the "regions beyond," but it had a more immediate meaning. Notice how Luke recorded the commission: "And ye shall be witnesses unto me both in Jerusalem, . . . and unto the uttermost part of the earth" (Acts 1:8).

The work was to begin at home. Assuredly there is a "story to tell to the nations," but the first responsibility is to tell the story in "Jerusalem," that is, at home. The home mission is a matter of "going" as well as the foreign mission.

Actually, the word "mission" is derived from the Latin, and it means to send. The word "visit" is also a Latin derivative and means to go. A missionary is one who is sent. A visitor is one who goes. These two words indicated two phases of the same task. Mission work requires visitation; visitation is mission work. The terms are synonymous in the final analysis. They are the Siamese twins of the gospel, inseparably related. A ministry of visitation is a missionary ministry. Furthermore, visitation in America is as much a missionary task as it would be in Africa or China. In the most exact sense of the word a Christian visitor is a missionary.

Jesus built his church to evangelize the world. He gave it a specific task in "Jerusalem," that is, in its own neighborhood. He gave it a plan of work, "Go ye." Christ's plan for his church and its members is therefore interpreted to be a ministry of personal and corporate visitation.

I. Visitation Was Established by the Heavenly Father

It has been said that no one ever understands anything well until he understands it historically. This fact should cause every Christian to make a thorough study of the vital ministry called visitation. It might well be called the Christian doctrine of work.

1. *It Began in the Garden of Eden*

Whence visitation? It originated in the heart and mind of God. It was first put into operation by God himself in the garden of Eden. It must have been a glorious experience for Adam and Eve when God came to visit with them in "the cool of the day." The indescribable beauty, the glories of a freshly created world, and the fellowship with the Creator himself must have been little short of heaven itself. It is not known how often God walked and talked with those whom he had made in his own image, but these were visits of joyful communion.

Even after Adam and Eve had fallen into sin and disobedience to God, he came to seek them out and cover their nakedness. Even though God was forced to expel them from the garden and punish them for their terrible sin, he promised them a Redeemer (Gen. 3:15). He who had all resources of the universe at his command chose to commune with those he loved by personal visitation!

2. *It Served as a Contact Between God and His People*

Throughout the long history of Israel, God continued to visit his creatures. It was his major method of communication with those whom he sought to reach. He visited Abraham frequently to prepare him to become the father of a great nation. He visited Moses at the burning bush and sent him to deliver his chosen people out of Egyptian bondage. He visited Moses again at Mount Sinai and delivered to him the tables of law which he had written with his own hand.

In the darkness of night he visited the boy Samuel to call him to be a prophet unto his people. He visited the prophet Isaiah and gave him a revelation of the coming Messiah. The entire Old Testament is aglow with the vivid accounts of divine visitation. This is the way God deigned to call upon his chosen people to chasten, to encourage, to deliver, and to succor them.

3. *It Was Culminated at Calvary*

The closing of the Old Testament inspiration did not mark the end of God's visitation program. Did not Calvary consummate the visit of all visits? Was not this the visit sublime? It was there that God gave himself, through the Son, to save the world. From that memorable day Christian visitation has been inseparably associated with salvation. It is, both in its origin and purpose, completely and gloriously a divine ministry.

II. VISITATION WAS THE METHOD OF THE LORD JESUS

"For unto you is born this day in the city of David a Saviour, which is Christ the Lord" (Luke 2:11). This brief statement announced the glorious and dramatic appearance of the Lord on this earth. It was the most phenomenal occurrence in history. It was the beginning of a visit! Christ had come from the heavenly mansions to make this world a remarkable visit. For some three and a half years he "went about all the cities and villages, teaching . . . preaching . . . healing" (Matt. 9:35).

1. *He Visited in the Homes of the People*

In each city and village Jesus went into the homes of the people. He performed his first miracle while visiting in a home. It was the miraculous transformation of water into wine at the marriage feast in Cana. He went into the home of Simon Peter and healed the mother-in-law. He went into the home of Levi and feasted with the publicans and sinners. He went into the home of one of the Pharisees, where he was found by the woman who washed his feet with her tears. His entire ministry was characterized by visiting in the homes of the people. His was truly a home ministry.

2. *He Sent His Disciples into the Homes of the People*

When Jesus first sent out the disciples, he specifically sent them into the homes of the people. His instructions were: "But go rather to the lost sheep of the house of Israel" (Matt. 10:6); "and when ye come into an house, salute it" (Matt. 10:12). Likewise, when he sent out the seventy, he expected them to go into the homes, for he gave them admonition as follows: "And into whatsoever house ye enter, first say, Peace be to this house" (Luke 10:5).

3. *He Made Wayside Visits*

As Jesus was journeying from Jericho to Jerusalem, he came upon two blind men sitting by the way. His compassionate heart was moved and he healed them. It was an act of mercy coming out of a chance contact along the way.

On another occasion while Jesus was on his way to visit Jairus, he paused long enough to heal a woman with an issue of blood. This wayside visit not only permitted him to cure a long-standing illness, but it gave him opportunity to cure a sin-sick soul.

4. *He Visited Specific Individuals*

While traveling from Judea to Galilee, Jesus felt that he must go through Samaria. He had a visit to make. Visitation was a divine necessity for Jesus. At noon he arrived at Jacob's well.

The one he had come to visit came to the well to draw water. She was a wicked woman of Samaria, yet her soul was priceless in the sight of the Lord. It is well to notice that Jesus arranged to make this visit alone. Her problems were too personal for observers. By dealing with this woman individually, Jesus was soon able to show her that the wells of this world would not satisfy a spiritual thirst.

Who would ever think of looking up in a tree for a contact? As Jesus entered Jericho, a little man hurriedly climbed a sycamore to get a better view of the Master. When Jesus came to the tree, he looked up and said unto him, "Zacchaeus, make haste, and come down; for to day I must abide at thy house" (Luke 19:5).

5. *He Visited Family Groups*

Jesus made frequent visits to the home of Mary, Martha, and Lazarus. These were more than social calls. They were for encouragement and inspiration. They were for instruction in the way of life. Jesus realized that the best results could be obtained by helping the entire household.

6. *He Visited the Crowded Places*

Although Jesus recognized the value of dealing with individuals and small groups, he was not an isolationist. He frequently sought the crowds. He mingled with the masses; he went where the people were. He did not wait for them to seek him; he sought them.

One day he joined the crowds along the shore of the Sea of Galilee. There he found Simon and Andrew casting their nets into the sea. After visiting with them, Jesus enlisted their help, and they forsook their nets to become fishers of men. Andrew became the first soul-winner and Simon Peter the great evangelist.

Another striking example is recorded in the fifth chapter of John. As Jesus stood looking upon the crowd of suffering humanity at the pool of Bethesda, he singled out the most helpless cripple of them all. With the simple question, "Wilt thou be made whole?" a contact was made. In a short time a man who had been crippled for many years walked away carrying his bed.

At another time Jesus appeared at the crowded tax office. Matthew, the "collector of internal revenue," was selected from that crowd. When the visit was concluded, the tax collector's office was short one capable Jew.

Jesus did not rest the success of his mission on a hit-and-miss proposition. He had a definite plan for his work. It was simply a matter of making a personal appeal. He sought out his prospect wherever he might be found. He secured interest, held the issue close to the individual's heart, and pressed for a decision. It is

certainly true that Jesus did his most effective work
through the ministry of visitation.

III. VISITATION WAS PRACTICED BY THE EARLY CHRISTIANS

The early Christians knew that visitation was God's
divine plan for reaching the people with the gospel.
They had seen Jesus visit. They knew that Jesus intended for them to go to every person they could find.
They realized that if they were to witness for Christ,
they must visit systematically.

The early Christians knew, even though the silent
testimony of a Christlike life was important, that few
people could be reached by wordless example. They
felt that the commission of Christ required more than
a life well-lived; it demanded a word well-spoken.
They not only believed that visitation was God's plan;
they practiced it consistently.

1. *Peter Believed in Visitation*

It is quite evident that Peter believed that he was
divinely obligated as a Christian to visit. He made
frequent visits in the homes of the people. Peter was
likely a frequent visitor in the home of Dorcas. When
she died, Peter was asked to come again, and God enabled him to raise her from the dead.

Peter visited the home of Cornelius, also. This visit
is of utmost significance, for as Peter preached here,
the gospel was made available to the Gentiles as well
as the Jews.

2. *John Preferred Visitation*

Although the beloved apostle John was particularly
effective as a writer, he was even more devoted to the

ministry of visitation. His abiding interest in this ministry is evidenced by his frequent references to it in his writings. For example, in 2 John 12 he wrote: "Having many things to write unto you, I would not write with paper and ink: but I trust to come unto you, and speak face to face, that our joy may be full." In writing to Gaius, he said: "But I trust I shall shortly see thee, and we shall speak face to face" (3 John 14).

3. *Paul Was a Consistent Visitor*

Paul was the greatest exponent and exemplar of visitation in New Testament times. He left a marvelous example for all visitors. It was his custom to go from house to house testifying and teaching about Christ.

Paul's own testimony is an unfailing challenge: "Ye know, from the first day that I came into Asia, after what manner I have been with you at all seasons, serving the Lord with all humility of mind, and with many tears, and temptations, which befell me by the lying in wait of the Jews: and how I kept back nothing that was profitable unto you, but have shewed you, and have taught you publicly, and from house to house, testifying both to the Jews, and also to the Greeks, repentance toward God, and faith toward our Lord Jesus Christ" (Acts 20:18-21).

IV. VISITATION WAS THE PROGRAM OF THE NEW TESTAMENT CHURCHES

Armitage, the historian, is quoted as follows: "By the close of the first century there were at least 500,000 believers." This phenomenal growth came about as a result of the faithfulness of those early New Testament churches in their visitation program. It is a fact

that visitation was the principal characteristic of those
churches.

1. *The Church at Jerusalem Had a Visitation Program*

At the beginning of this church, the number of members was quite insignificant. It had no more than 120
members when Jesus returned to the Father. But
something happened! This small band of believers
continued with one accord in prayer and in daily witnessing from house to house all over Jerusalem.

Strangely enough, or rather properly enough, the
leaders in the visitation program of the Jerusalem
church were laymen. The deacons led out in the
matter, and everyone participated. The pastor, or
pastors, are not even mentioned in regard to this
program.

Stephen and Philip seemed to be the ones in charge
of the work. Because of the tireless efforts of these
two great deacons and their co-laborers, the gospel was
carried to every nook and corner of Jerusalem. Their
success was colossal.

It was inevitable that the enemies of Christ and his
church be stirred up. Unbelievable persecutions ensued. These trials brought about the death of Stephen,
the scattering abroad of the other workers, and the
discouragement of the few left in Jerusalem.

This persecution could easily have been the end of
the Jerusalem church, but it was not so. Not only
did those who were scattered witness for Christ, but
those who were allowed to remain in Jerusalem were
also faithful in keeping up their visitation. The result
was that, in spite of the dreadful persecutions, this
church grew to an unbelievable size.

2. *The Church at Antioch Was Established as a Result of Visitation*

A great revival swept through Antioch with many being reached with the gospel, both Jews and Gentiles. The reason for this revival is not given in the Scriptures, but it is reasonable to suppose that it came even as revivals come today. Some of the members of the Jerusalem church must have fled to Antioch, immediately giving themselves to personal visitation in the homes. In this way people heard of Christ, and a great revival began.

Reports of the revival in Antioch reached the mother church in Jerusalem. This was an unexpected development, so Barnabas was chosen to investigate the work. After arriving in Antioch, Barnabas was so impressed with the opportunities that he immediately set out for Tarsus to secure the help of Paul. Paul and Barnabas remained in Antioch for a full year to help build up and organize the new church which had been born in a flaming spirit of evangelism.

The conquering spirit of these visiting Christians was not to be satisfied in Antioch alone. There were multitudes to the west who had never heard the gospel message. They, too, must be reached. Paul and Barnabas were set apart for this task, and the first missionary effort was launched.

The work of these two outstanding leaders was largely a matter of visiting, teaching, and witnessing. Today's mission is the same; it is still visiting, teaching, and witnessing. Those who practice it today are genuinely missionary both in heart and in spirit, whether they do it at home or abroad.

The other missionary efforts of the church at Antioch, particularly those of Paul, were not an independent, disjointed "series of meetings" designed to pay the traveling expenses of Paul and his traveling companions. They were Spirit-directed visitation efforts of the church. The entire purpose was to preach Christ abroad as well as at home. The Antioch Christians were so elated over their visitation work at home that they felt a divine compulsion to share with those in other regions.

3. *The Church at Philippi Was a Monument to the Effectiveness of Visitation*

This church was the result of a visit made by Paul in answer to the call to "come over into Macedonia, and help us" (Acts 16:9).

4. *The Churches at Rome Were Zealous in Visitation*

Probably there were three churches already in existence in Rome before Paul arrived. It is thought that some of Paul's kinsmen were converted under the ministry of Stephen and that they fled to Rome when Paul began his bitter persecutions. (See Rom. 16:7.) Doubtless many Romans were also converted at Pentecost, and they returned home to tell their neighbors.

It is not certain just what part visitation played in the establishment of these churches. It seems logical that they were also the result of visitation. At this time in history the zeal of the Christians for visitation was at its zenith, and there is little doubt but that the churches in Rome were established and developed through an organized program of visitation.

In a matter of ten years, or less, several churches had been established through visitation. The number of new churches, plus the unprecedented growth in membership, is evidence that Christ's method of reaching people brought about the development of visitation as an integral part of the church program. New Testament churches practiced this principle of visitation diligently.

V. VISITATION WAS A FACTOR IN THE REMARKABLE SPREAD OF CHRISTIANITY

It is difficult to realize how remarkably fast Christianity spread in those early years. Just a hint may be found in the Bible: "Therefore they that were scattered abroad went every where preaching the word" (Acts 8:4). Although it required persecution to get the early believers started on their program of visitation, it is most significant that they told the good news of the gospel everywhere.

As the persecutions drove them abroad, these witnesses went from house to house as living firebrands setting souls on fire and turning the world upside down for Christ. It was not a matter for the preachers to discharge. It was the work of every member. If every believer today would witness for Christ as those early believers did, the results would be beyond comprehension.

1. *Visitation Won Half of the World's Population in a Short Time*

When one realizes that every believer was a constant witness to Christ, it is understandable how half of the then known world was won to Christ. The historian, Tertullian (A.D. 160-222), in speaking of this rapid growth of Christianity, said, "We are of yesterday, yet we have filled your empire, your cities, your towns, your islands, your tribes, your camps, castles, palaces, assemblies, and senate."

The growth was so widespread that in less than one hundred years there were as many as half a million

Christians scattered through Asia Minor and Western Europe. There were many others in Africa, England, and Wales by this time. By the time the imperial persecutions ended in A.D. 313, Christians numbered as much as half the entire population of the Roman Empire. Faithfulness in visitation is the only conceivable reason for this success, humanly speaking.

2. *Visitation Built Enormous Church Memberships*

Not only did the visitation work of the early churches win a large proportion of the world to Christ, but it was a significant factor also in the building of churches under the most trying circumstances. It would be most interesting to trace the growth of all these churches, but the Jerusalem church will suffice.

Recall how the two followers of John the Baptist believed that Jesus was the Messiah. Each sought out and won his own brother. It was through the efforts of these four—Andrew, Peter, James, and John—that Philip was won. Philip in turn sought out Nathanael, and soon the group had grown to twelve.

The multiplication of believers became so rapid that the Jerusalem church soon had not only the "seventy" but 120. The ministry of Peter and those associated with him quickly accounted for three thousand. Acts 4:4 records that there were five thousand men alone by this time. Acts 6:7 avows that "the number of the disciples multiplied in Jerusalem greatly."

Most church historians agree that this church membership grew to twenty or twenty-five thousand. Some think it had as many as fifty thousand members. Dr. B. H. Carroll went so far as to say that it reached a membership of one hundred thousand. Unquestionably this church had several times as many members as the largest of present-day churches.

Just how did the Jerusalem church reach so many people? They were not reached because of a beautiful cathedral, marvelous music, or a magnetic pastor. Their pastor was a plain man; they had no outstanding music program. They did not even have a building in which to worship, for apparently the first church building was erected during the reign of Alexander Severus, A.D. 222-235.

The Jerusalem church is the outstanding example of what a good visitation program can accomplish. If it could build a membership counted in the multiplied thousands, without a building or equipment, just what could be done by a church with all the marvelous provisions of the present time?

Churches which are not fortunate enough to have good equipment may take heart. They should realize that visitation built the largest church the world has ever known; yet it had no place in which to worship and no equipment with which to work!

FOR CLASS DISCUSSION

Do you agree with the author's estimate of the emphasis which the Bible gives to visitation? In your consideration, take into account the following definition of the Greek word translated "visit" in the New Testament: "to go to see, to relieve" (From Strong's *Exhaustive Concordance of the Bible*).

Plan together to combine actual visitation and reports with your study of this book.

CHAPTER 2

I. MAKE VISITATION A MATTER OF CHURCH POLICY

II. SCHEDULE WEEKLY VISITATION DAY

III. ASK THE PASTOR TO SUPERVISE THE VISITATION PROGRAM

IV. SECURE A SUPERINTENDENT OF ENLARGEMENT TO LEAD THE VISITATION PROGRAM
1. He Should Be Elected by the Church
2. He Should Be Fitted for the Task

V. PREPARE AND MAINTAIN A MASTER FILE OF PROSPECTS
1. Take a Religious Census
2. Examine the Church Membership Roll
3. Contact Those Who Sign Visitors' Cards in the Church Services
4. Check the Homes of Those Already Enrolled in Sunday School
5. Secure Lists of Names Which Are Prepared for Business Concerns

VI. FOLLOW A CONCERTED PLAN OF VISITATION
1. Consider the Advantages of the Concerted Plan
2. Set Up a Comprehensive Schedule

II

Developing a Systematic Program of Visitation

Two thousand years have come and gone since Jesus left his command to disciple the world. Yet there are multiplied thousands who have never heard the gospel story. What is wrong? Is the plan of God inadequate for the task? Is it too idealistic? The fault does not lie in God's plan of work. The actual difficulty is that the plan has not been properly used by many churches.

Although much progress has been made in recent years in returning to God's plan for reaching people, there is still much to be done. It is true that visitation has always characterized successful churches. Nevertheless, many churches today are making little progress in their communities largely because they have no practical plan for getting into the homes of the people. Some have depended entirely upon the worship services or the annual revival for reaching new people. Others have depended upon Christian fellowship as a substitute for visitation, forgetting that filling church buildings is contingent upon going out after the people.

In spite of the many scriptural injunctions to "go," and regardless of the example of the early churches, visitation is the one major task which churches most frequently bungle or ignore completely. What can be done to give visitation its proper emphasis and to get it into the life of a church? How may a church develop a systematic program of visitation?

I. MAKE VISITATION A MATTER OF CHURCH POLICY

Baptist churches have policies on church government, doctrine, ordinances, finance, discipline, membership, and many other things. It is only logical that they have a policy for finding and enlisting the unreached masses. A church would do well to adopt a visitation policy similar to the following and spread it on the minutes of the church:

CHURCH POLICY ON VISITATION

WHEREAS, We believe that the command of our Lord to go into all the world applies specifically to our local community, and,

WHEREAS, We believe that only a comprehensive program of house-to-house visitation can accomplish his purpose,

Be it hereby resolved—

1. That regular, systematic visitation be given a major place in our church life and program.

2. That a superintendent of enlargement be elected by the church to plan and direct the visitation of the Sunday school.

3. That the absentees be contacted every week by the persons assigned such duties.

4. That a master file of all prospects be set up and made available.

5. That regular assignments of prospects be made to all officers and teachers and to as many other members as possible.

6. That definite reports be made on all visitation.

7. That unsaved persons be given full priority in visitation.

Done by order of the church in regular business session.

_____Date _____Clerk

II. SCHEDULE WEEKLY VISITATION DAY

A "visit when you can" policy is too haphazard to get the best results. There must be a definite day, definite hour, and definite place if visitation is to be thoroughly effective. This means that each church should set aside a day for visitation in its calendar of activities.

The most appropriate day should be selected and observed as regularly as prayer meeting. Nothing else should be allowed on the church calendar for that day. Any day will be good so long as the majority can fit into the schedule. The latter part of the week is generally conceded to be the most effective because of its nearness to the Lord's Day. Probably more churches use Thursday than any other day.

There will not likely be a time when all the visitors can go, but a suitable time may be found for the majority of them.

III. ASK THE PASTOR TO SUPERVISE THE VISITATION PROGRAM

Visitation is a major task of the church; therefore the church is obligated to give direction and supervision to the work. Who is responsible for such direction? Some larger churches are fortunate enough to have staff members for this task, but the majority of the churches will have to depend upon the pastor to direct the work. Actually the task belongs to the pastor as the undershepherd of God. Is it not true that the pastor is responsible to God for the full administration of his church? He must lead, vitalize, and inspirit the visitors of his church.

Some may feel that the pastor is too busy. Indeed, he is too busy if he is not giving attention and direction to the major items in his church program. Likely there is no busier pastor in all the world than Dr. Robert G. Lee, Bellevue Baptist Church, Memphis, Tennessee. In a recent ten-year period Dr. Lee made a total of 36,500 personal visits. That is an average of ten per day for ten years! Probably no other pastor has ever equaled that record. It is no wonder that for a generation Dr. Lee has baptized candidates every Sunday he has been in his pulpit.

It is a fallacy to say that the pastor must do all the visiting, but it is likewise folly to excuse him from his responsibility.

IV. SECURE A SUPERINTENDENT OF ENLARGEMENT TO LEAD THE VISITATION PROGRAM

The importance of visitation demands regular supervision. The most capable person available should be elected as superintendent of enlargement and given the responsibility to promote the visitation program.

1. *He Should Be Elected by the Church*

The church should select and elect a person to direct the work of visitation. He should be called the superintendent of enlargement. As such he will be a general officer of the Sunday school. He will bear the responsibility of planning, administering, and inspiriting the visitation efforts of the school. In most cases he should hold no other church office.

2. *He Should Be Fitted for the Task*

It will be necessary for the superintendent of enlargement to deal directly with all the department superintendents, teachers, and class officers. He should therefore be well prepared by experience and careful study for the task involved.

(1) He must be a born-again, consecrated member of the church.

(2) He must be a person of unquestionable loyalties.

(3) He should be conversant with his church and denominational program of work and should be heartily in accord with it.

(4) He should be an efficient and successful visitor.

(5) He should possess a winsome and forceful personality.

(6) He should be able to work with people and to inspire their co-operation.

(7) He should be capable of working out and projecting definite plans of work.

(8) He should know the duties of all department and class officers who are charged with visitation.

V. PREPARE AND MAINTAIN A MASTER FILE OF PROSPECTS

A comprehensive visitation program requires a constant source of prospective members. This can be obtained by preparing and maintaining a master file of prospects. This is a duty of the enlargement superintendent. Supplies and card forms for this purpose may be secured from the Baptist Book Store serving your area.

The master file should include the names of all the prospects. These names may be secured in various ways:

1. *Take a Religious Census*

The best place to find prospects is in their own homes. It is impossible to do this without at least an annual census of the church territory. Details for taking a religious census can be found in Arthur Flake's *Building a Standard Sunday School*, chapter 3. A brief outline of the procedure is as follows:

(1) Decide upon the territory to be covered.

(2) Arrange the territory by districts according to streets, roads, or sections.

(3) Enlist district captains and census workers equal to the task.

(4) Provide the census envelopes, cards, and other materials.

(5) Instruct and train the workers.

(6) Send out the census takers at the appointed time.

(7) Check the census cards against the church roll, Sunday school roll, and prospect files.

(8) Grade and classify all prospects according to age.

(9) List and tabulate all the information.

2. *Examine the Church Membership Roll*

Approximately half of the membership in the average church is not enrolled in Sunday school. They rarely ever attend the worship services or show in any way that they belong. Even though their names are on the church roll, they are in every sense of the word "prospects." Actually these church members are a liability, but they constitute a great opportunity. They need to be enlisted rather than neglected. They need prayer and sympathetic help rather than criticism.

The vast majority of them can be reached if the church so desires.

Some churches have reached every resident member for Bible study; even large churches have done so. Every church and Sunday school would do well to remember that the unenlisted church member is a priority prospect.

3. Contact Those Who Sign Visitors' Cards in the Church Services

Some of the very best prospects are to be found among those who visit in the churches. They already have an interest in the church if they come to visit. Special recognition of these visitors should be made in all services. This is only a gesture of Christian friendliness; yet it provides many prospects.

The wise use of visitors' cards will invariably result in identifying interested persons. It is unforgivable to ignore the visitors. Nothing turns people away from a church so quickly as being ignored in the services. Many good churches are guilty of this oversight.

Sunday school classes will also find valuable prospects among those persons who visit their classes from time to time. The class officers should give special recognition and attention to such visitors.

4. Check the Homes of Those Already Enrolled in Sunday School

"Buried treasure" can often be found in the homes of those already enrolled in Sunday school. Many adult prospects can be found among the parents of the children. Brothers and sisters and often other relatives live within the same home, yet they do not attend Sunday school or church. Frequently prospects may be discovered among those who rent rooms in these homes.

5. *Secure Lists of Names Which Are Prepared for Business Concerns*

Practically every community has commercial lists published regularly. The information found on these lists generally includes the following: (1) newcomers, (2) local moves, (3) births, (4) deaths, (5) church affiliation, etc. Every church would be wise to secure these lists. They are ordinarily secured from the utility companies, chamber of commerce, better business bureau, "welcome wagon," etc.

Each church should designate certain persons to make an initial contact with prospects found on these lists. Complete information should be secured and written reports made. Some of the larger churches employ a full-time worker to care for this important matter. A volunteer worker could perform this valuable service in the smaller churches.

The prospects found in this manner are frequently easy to reach. They are strangers in a new community and are lonesome for some friendly gesture.

VI. FOLLOW A CONCERTED PLAN OF VISITATION

Many churches have tried various plans of visitation. However, many of them have not been too successful because they lacked a unity of effort. Co-operation in visitation, as in all phases of Baptist church life, is essential to success.

1. *Consider the Advantages of the Concerted Plan*

The concerted plan of action has been proved over and over to be the most practical and effective plan.

(1) *It is scriptural.*—The New Testament Christians gave themselves to visitation, "and daily . . . in every house, they ceased not to teach and preach Jesus

Christ" (Acts 5:42). They worked together. After meeting for prayer and fellowship, they departed to witness to the saving power of Jesus.

Such a period of meditation and preparation is just as helpful to the present-day visitor. To join with those of kindred spirit and purpose for a brief period of preparation puts the visitors in a better frame of mind, encourages the weakhearted, and greatly improves the quality of the visitation done.

(2) *It inspires the visitors.*—It is easy to become discouraged and disappointed when one attempts to visit alone and without preparation. There is a decided lift in fellowshiping with those who are preparing to do the same thing at the same time. The flame of enthusiasm burns brightest when there are great groups of people going out into the highways and hedges together.

(3) *It magnifies visitation.*—When the concerted plan of visitation is used, it places visitation on a higher plane. It is given the proper time and place that visitation deserves. Concerted visitation commands the respect and attention of the community. The task which receives so much time and attention of the church members will make a significant impact upon the community.

(4) *It saves time.*—Most Christians fail to visit because they think they do not have the time. A regular time for visitation makes possible a sensible budgeting of time both for the individual and the church. A busy life and a heavy church program, in some cases, leave one with a sense of frustration. This difficult situation may be greatly alleviated by having a definite time set aside for the ministry of visitation. A concerted effort also guarantees that time will be saved by avoiding conflicts in personal and church schedules.

2. *Set Up a Comprehensive Schedule*

In some cases it might be impractical to gather in the
church before and/or after visitation. It certainly
leaves much to be desired, however, if this is not done.
The best results in visitation are secured when all
the visitors meet at the church for prayer and instruction before going out to visit. At this very brief
meeting, assignments should be verified, advertising
media given out, transportation arranged, and thorough
preparation made.

The concerted plan deserves a full day. Nothing else
should be scheduled for that day in the church calendar. This will enable all the workers to do their
part in making the plan work. A schedule for the day
is essential. The following one is working splendidly
in many churches large and small:

9:30 A.M. Workers with the preschool age children,
Cradle Roll and Extension workers, and the teachers
and class officers of the Adult women's classes meet at
the church. Prayer is offered, instructions given, and
assignments verified before the workers go out on the
field.

3:00 P.M. All workers with school-age children meet
in the same type meeting and go out to visit the boys
and girls as they arrive home from school. This part of
the program may be moved to the 9:30 A.M. hour during
the summer months.

7:00 P.M. All workers with the Young People's and
Adult men's classes, the class officers, plus any other
workers who are employed away from the home, can
come at this hour for preparation and visitation. This
particular hour makes definite provision for visitation
by the men. Many classes will want to return to the
church or go to some other place for reports and fellowship.

A church cannot take too seriously its task of reaching more people for Bible study. The following story, a dream related by Dr. J. B. Rounds, is an indictment against the visitation program of the average church:

"An almost endless line of people crowded before the church. Such an unusual sight aroused the curiosity of a preacher. After making several inquiries, he discovered that no one really knew why the great crowd was seeking to get inside the church. He, too, joined the crowd and waited in line to get inside. Eventually he made his way up the steps and down the aisle to the front of the church. The most amazing spectacle imaginable captured his attention. There, chained to the pulpit of the great church, was the Lord Jesus Christ! In astonishment the preacher asked: 'Lord, what is the meaning of this? Why are you chained to this pulpit?'

"The Lord replied sorrowfully: 'My people have done this to me. Instead of following my command to go tell the world the good news of salvation, they have chained me to this pulpit and only those who are interested enough to come in ever hear about me.' "

"Go out into the highways and hedges, and compel them to come in" (Luke 14:23)

FOR CLASS DISCUSSION

Evaluate the visitation program of your church in the light of this chapter. What words of commendation would you like to give your pastor and other workers who direct the program? What suggestions for improvement would you like to offer?

CHAPTER 3

I. Maintain a Permanent Visitation Program

II. Give Adequate Publicity
   1. Use the Church Bulletin
   2. Employ Visual Aids
   3. Make Announcements from the Pulpit

III. Prepare Definite Visitation Assignments
   1. Make Absentee Assignments
   2. Make Prospect Assignments
   3. Make Faithful Member Assignments

IV. Secure Adequate Reports
   1. Use Written Reports
   2. Call for Testimonials
   3. Recognize the Faithful Visitors

V. Train the Visitors Carefully
   1. Observe Successful Visitors
   2. Provide Special Weeks of Study
   3. Give Instruction at the Time of Visitation

VI. Inspirit the Visitors

III

Making the Visitation Program Effective

I T is entirely possible to set up a program of visitation that is mechanically perfect and yet lacking in effectiveness. Effectiveness requires more than catchy slogans or enthusiastic exhortations, although these are helpful.

There are many factors which determine the efficiency of the visitation program. Meticulous planning is vitally involved. The need for real leadership is unparalleled. Making the visitation program effective is a task that will require earnest prayer, careful study, hard work, and constant attention.

The qualifications of the superintendent of enlargement have been discussed in the preceding chapter. However, it should be further emphasized here that he is directly responsible for the success of the visitation program. How can this be accomplished?

I. MAINTAIN A PERMANENT VISITATION PROGRAM

Effective visitation requires constant and aggressive attention. Periodic emphasis upon visitation will not suffice. The emphasis must be an unwavering force. If vigorously promoted, even a poor visitation program will be somewhat effective. A permanent program

backed by the entire Sunday school will accomplish
the best results.

The multitudes of unenlisted people demand a continuous effort. Anything that approaches a worthy
plan must operate every week of the year, not just
during a revival meeting, in the spring or summer, or
at convenient seasons. It must be as much a part of
the church program and as regular as the prayer meeting or Sunday worship services.

II. GIVE ADEQUATE PUBLICITY

One of the best ways to make visitation effective
is to advertise and publicize it regularly. If visitation
is not important enough to keep before the people,
it is not important enough to do. How may the
visitation work of the Sunday school be given its
proper place in the church publicity?

1. *Use the Church Bulletin*

Although the church bulletin is strictly impersonal
publicity, it is in many respects the most valuable advertising in the church field. Since the bulletin is
a news organ of the church, it certainly should be
used to promote visitation. Visitation should be a
major interest and concern of the church, so it is
only fitting that a generous part of the church advertising be given to this matter.

2. *Employ Visual Aids*

There are many forms of visual aids which may be
used to promote visitation. Posters, show cards, signs,
letters, banners, newspaper articles, skits, and demonstrations only begin to be suggestive of the possibilities
in this part of the advertising field. There should

always be something to be seen around the church to keep visitation before the people.

3. *Make Announcements from the Pulpit*

Some few persons might object to using the pulpit to publicize visitation. Probably this is because they have not given proper consideration to the importance of the ministry of visitation. How could it be incongruous to magnify and promote the very thing which characterized the entire ministry of Jesus? All promotional efforts would, of course, be carried out with dignity and dispatch. When this is done, it will not detract from the worship service, but will make a definite contribution.

III. PREPARE DEFINITE VISITATION ASSIGNMENTS

Visitation that is not definitely assigned is rarely effective. Few visitors are successful who visit without a particular person in mind and a clear purpose in view. This requires regular assignments.

There are three groups which deserve visitation by the Sunday school: first, the absentees; second, the prospects; and third, the regular members. Each one of these groups needs to be definitely assigned to visitors. The assignments may be made in various ways. Some churches have a post card form on which assignments are made and mailed to the visitors. Others use a visitation assignment board. Some make the assignments on Sunday morning. Others telephone the assignments to the visitors.

It seems that the best time for making assignments is the weekly officers and teachers' meeting. Since visitation is an outgrowth of Bible teaching, this meeting provides an excellent opportunity for keeping this relationship clear. Attention to absentees and prospects should be a regular part of the weekly teachers' meeting.

1. *Make Absentee Assignments*

Absentee visits are the definite responsibility of the class. The teacher is responsible for seeing that the class officers are faithful in this duty. The teacher will not shirk the visitation of absentees but will cooperate fully in this work.

In most churches the class secretary makes a list of the absentees from the records, and the list is ready at the conclusion of the class period. In some Sunday schools the department secretary makes these lists. Some churches, both large and small, feel that the matter is so important that they have a complete list of all absentees compiled in the church office each week. This is to guarantee that every visitor shall have a definite assignment for absentee visiting.

Assignments from the absentee lists are made on Wednesday evening at the weekly officers and teachers' meeting. This keeps the matter of absentees before the workers during the week. It helps create an absentee consciousness.

2. *Make Prospect Assignments*

Following the securing of the name of a possible prospect through a census or otherwise, an initial visit should be made to determine the accuracy of the preliminary information. The names of those found to be prospects are placed in the master file and a copy of the information is given to the proper teacher.

From week to week the superintendent of enlargement will make assignments from this file for visitation. He will need to observe the following procedure in making the assignments:

(1) *Use a written assignment slip.*—Assignment
forms are available at the Baptist Book Stores. These
forms provide for the full information on each individual similar to the census: name, date of birth, spiritual condition, church membership, special observations
to be recorded by the visitor, and other valuable information.

(2) *Set up a working file for cards of prospects
being assigned each week.*—When assignments are made
each week, the superintendent of enlargement should
transfer the prospect cards from the master file to a
working file. The working file would consist of cards
with tabs labeled for each week of the month: 1st week,
2nd week, 3rd week, 4th week, 5th week. Master-file
cards for prospects assigned the first week would be
placed behind the tab labeled "3rd week" in the working file; cards for assignments made the second week
would be placed behind the tab labeled "4th week,"
and so on.

In other words each visitor would be given two weeks
to make the contact. If reports are not turned in the
same week the assignment is received, the visit has
probably not been made. The superintendent of enlargement will simply reassign the name when the two
weeks have elapsed. This system prevents his having
to track down every visitor to secure a report. If the
visit is made the same week the assignment is given and
the report is turned in, the prospect card is removed
from the working file, the results of the visit recorded
and the card restored to the master prospect file.

3. *Make Faithful Member Assignments*

Visitation of the "faithfuls" is too often overlooked.
In the rush to see prospects and absentees, the "back-
bone" members are easily forgotten. These faithful

persons deserve some time and attention from the class
as well as from the teacher. A visit to express a word
of appreciation for faithful attendance is quite in order.
This shows that the teacher is interested in more than
just building up the class attendance. Equally important is a visit to all class members certainly within the
first two or three months after promotion.

IV. SECURE ADEQUATE REPORTS

More visitation is done when reports are required.
Perhaps it is poor motivation to require reports, but
it helps get the workers started. Many good visitors
have been developed and have grown spiritually because of the gentle persuasion of reports.

Variety in making reports is most helpful. There
must be nothing dull and prosaic about them. They
should be vibrant and enthusiastic because they repre-
sent human souls. How can reports on visitation be
made?

1. *Use Written Reports*

As previously noted, most assignments for visitation
are made on card forms. This makes written reports
an easy matter since the report can be made on the
reverse side of the assignment card.

Written reports should always be made in the weekly
meeting of the officers and teachers. The record system for this meeting provides a report space for all
visits. A large blackboard is also useful in making
reports either by classes or departments. A monthly
review and report of the visitation done by the entire
Sunday school can be readily compiled from the written
reports.

2. *Call for Testimonials*

The tenth chapter of Luke records the sending out of

the seventy.   Luke 10:17 constitutes the report they made upon their return. It is a testimony to the effectiveness of visitation. Notice that they returned with joy.

There is no joy quite like that of those returning from the harvest fields to report on their visitation experiences. It is always inspiring and thrilling to hear the glowing reports of the blessings of God. They are effective incentives in leading others to visit. Testimonies are also most helpful in encouraging a discouraged visitor.

3. Recognize the Faithful Visitors

A sincere visitor does not work for recognition. Nevertheless, those who give of their time in visitation deserve and ought to receive recognition for their faithfulness. Both public and private expressions of appreciation will encourage the workers to keep at the task faithfully.

It is true that those who are doing this work are doing no more than they should do; however, when one considers the large number who ought to be visiting and are not doing so, it certainly seems in order to recognize those who are doing the work.

V. TRAIN THE VISITORS CAREFULLY

It is easy to consider the ability to do effective visitation as a gift when in reality it is an ability which has been gained through tedious effort. Success in the visitation art comes as it does in any other of the fine arts. It is a matter of careful training, patient practice, and prayerful dedication.

Any Christian can learn to visit acceptably, and he is obligated to do so. His church, however, is just as deeply obligated to train him how to visit.   There are many ways in which this training may be given.

1. *Observe Successful Visitors*

Jesus realized the importance of observation in learning how to visit. He made it a practice to visit in the presence of his disciples. He sent his workers out two by two so that they might have the advantage of learning from each other. This does not necessarily mean that all visitation must be done in the company of some other person. There are many visits that need to be made by a lone visitor.

Watching an accomplished visitor is one of the most effective ways of learning the art. It is a short-cut as well. Inexperienced visitors should be assigned to an experienced visitor for a period of observation. The more accomplished visitor should consider it a privilege to coach the beginner. Many wonderful experiences and blessings will come to those who assist others in learning how to visit effectively for Christ.

2. *Provide Special Weeks of Study*

Occasionally there should be a week of intensive study of the ministry of visitation. This week of study might be in the form of a training course. The scriptural, historical, and practical aspects of visitation should be given due consideration.

The major emphasis will be upon the methods of visitation. The manner of approaching the prospect, guiding the conversation, making an appeal, etc. all need to be thoroughly mastered. Demonstrations and discussions will need to be utilized. This will necessitate the selection of a competent teacher well in advance of the time for study.

Laboratory experience should be gained during this week of study. At least one visit should be assigned each day to each class member. Reports on the assignment and the success of the methods suggested should be made. Evaluations of the procedures used will prove helpful to the visitors and to those who hear the reports.

3. *Give Instruction at the Time of Visitation*

No church has a right to expect its members to visit unless it provides regular instruction for the visitors. When the concerted plan of visitation is used, the visitors meet for prayer and instruction before going on the field. Of course, the period of instruction will of necessity be brief. However, this is a most appropriate time for studying the art of visitation. After a few moments of devotional meditation a competent instructor should provide fresh and pertinent suggestions for effective visitation. This instruction may be given by the pastor or the superintendent of enlargement.

VI. INSPIRIT THE VISITORS

The most fruitful visitation is prompted by love. It is energized by the Holy Spirit. It springs from a heart of compassion. Fortunately, these high motives can be developed in the hearts of Christians. This may be done by presenting the challenge faced, by reviewing the commands of the Scriptures, and by magnifying the condition of those who are lost. These matters, coupled with a love of Christ and a desire to do the will of the Father, will keep visitors enthusiastic.

FOR CLASS DISCUSSION

Many visitation programs make a fine start, then "bog down." What suggestions in this chapter would help to keep your program going year in and year out?

CHAPTER 4

I. ACQUIRE WHOLESOME ATTITUDES TOWARD VISITATION
1. Establish Correct Mental Attitudes
2. Possess Proper Spiritual Attitudes
3. Evaluate Present Attitudes

II. CULTIVATE ESSENTIAL PERSONALITY TRAITS
1. Develop Spiritual-Mindedness
2. Practice Patience
3. Use Tact
4. Be Courageous
5. Employ Persistence
6. Inject Friendliness
7. Show Sympathy
8. Guard Confidences

III. MAKE PERSONAL PREPARATION
1. Present a Pleasing Appearance
2. Have Normal Health
3. Display a Pleasant Personality

IV. MAKE MENTAL PREPARATION
1. Determine the Objective of the Visit
2. Consider the Individual
3. Be Informed
4. Use the Excuses

V. MAKE SPIRITUAL PREPARATION
1. Pray Before Going
2. Exercise Faith
3. Go in the Strength of the Lord

IV

Qualifying as a Visitor

ANY normal person who knows the Lord as Saviour and who loves people has the basic qualifications necessary to becoming a successful visitor. However, these qualifications are only the beginning place. There are certain attitudes which must be acquired; there are essential aspects of personality which must be cultivated; there are specific areas in which preparation must be made. These are the things which actually qualify one as a visitor.

The first step in achieving these qualities is a realization of one's personal deficiency. The second step is a thorough study of the essential qualities. This should be followed by a determined attempt at personal improvement.

Such a procedure should not be discouraging. Rather it should be viewed as a sure road to better work. It should serve as an inspiration while one is striving to become a competent visitor.

I. ACQUIRE WHOLESOME ATTITUDES TOWARD VISITATION

The visitor's success depends in a great measure upon his attitudes toward visitation. Wholesome attitudes will help the visitor clarify his motives for visitation. They will make the difference between his being a duty-driven or love-impelled visitor.

1. *Establish Correct Mental Attitudes*

The correct mental attitude is fundamental in qualifying as a visitor. This is because one's attitude determines his manner of thinking, feeling, and acting. It would be impossible to be a successful visitor if one looked upon visitation as a drudgery or as an incidental matter.

Dr. Robert G. Lee must have been thinking in the realm of attitudes when he said, "Look on visitation as a business, not an incidental matter; as work, not play; as time well spent, not wasted; as a privilege, not a boresome duty."

2. *Possess Proper Spiritual Attitudes*

What spiritual attitudes are necessary in qualifying as a visitor?

A sincere desire to do the will of the Father is basic. It is this attitude which keeps the visitor's work from becoming shallow and superficial.

The recognition of Christ as supreme Lord of life is another spiritual attitude which the visitor should possess. It is this attitude which gives the visitor a genuine concern for others.

3. *Evaluate Present Attitudes*

An honest answer to each of the following questions will help the visitor evaluate his attitudes toward visitation as well as indicate the areas in which improvement is needed.

(1) Am I a messenger of peace and good will or a "glad hander" for my class?

QUALIFYING AS A VISITOR

(2) Am I representing Christ or simply seeking to discharge the obligations of an office?

(3) Am I more interested in helping people or in performing a duty?

(4) Am I rendering a spiritual service or making a professional or social call?

(5) Am I seeking to enlist people in Bible study or merely to bring an increase in attendance?

(6) Am I concerned with improving the spiritual status of the people or with making a report on absentees?

(7) Am I following in the footsteps of the Master or backing up my superintendent?

(8) Am I seeking to carry out the Great Commission or simply seeking to be efficient?

II. CULTIVATE ESSENTIAL PERSONALITY TRAITS

Not only does the successful visitor need the proper attitudes toward the work, but he must also seek to cultivate certain personal qualities. It is rather ironical that these traits are essential to good visitation and at the same time can be gained only through constant practice. This must not dishearten the visitor because every visit helps him to become more proficient in his art. The earnest cultivation of certain personality traits will assure one of becoming a master visitor.

1. Develop Spiritual-Mindedness

Visitation is inherently a spiritual function. It requires spiritual energy. This is why the real objectives of visitation cannot be gained except by spiritually minded persons.

Spiritual-mindedness is a rare quality. It is not the

natural tendency of man. It must be developed by Bible study, prayer, meditation, and wholehearted devotion to the Lord's cause.

2. *Practice Patience*

Patience has been defined as "waiting with love and expectancy." It is the quality of character which keeps the visitor at the task at all seasons. Patience will keep one going back even in the face of apparent defeat. It will help one suffer indifference or even rebuke in a Christian manner. In short, patience is power.

3. *Use Tact*

Dale Carnegie once said, "If you want to gather honey, don't kick over the beehive."

Tact is the peculiar skill of saying or doing the right thing required by the circumstances. It is spiritual intelligence. Knowing how to tackle successfully any problem begins with knowing what to say and how to say it.

4. *Be Courageous*

Timidity and fear are the two major enemies of the visitor. They are the most effective tools which Satan has to use. Courage comes from a complete faith in one's mission and from utter dependence upon the One who instituted the mission. Paul raised an unanswerable question, "If God be for us, who can be against us?" (Rom. 8:31). God's admonition to Joshua should become the motto of every visitor: "Only be thou strong and very courageous" (Josh. 1:7).

5. *Employ Persistence*

A quiet persistence is an essential trait of the good visitor. There is no time nor place to quit in the business of seeking those who need God. The difference between success and failure often lies right here. The

very next visit may be the one which decides the issue.
What if that visit were never made? The persistent
visitor will keep on going even when the prospect says
he is not interested. The persistent visitor will go lovingly, kindly, tenderly, until the prospect is enlisted.

The author once selected one hundred prospects
from a census for a test of the effectiveness of his Sunday school workers. An accurate record of all visits
made to these prospects was kept. It was found that
some were enlisted on the first visit, others on the
second or third visit, and some were more difficult to
enlist. The last one of the prospects was enlisted five
years later. It took an average of thirteen visits to
reach those one hundred prospects. How many visitors
would ever go thirteen times to the same prospect?

It may be that some prospects cannot be enlisted;
nevertheless, God honors the faithful visitor by sending in those who have not been visited. This fact may
be expressed in an axiom of visitation: "We visit a
lot of people we never get, but we get a lot of people
we never visit; but we'd never get a lot of people we
never visit if we didn't visit a lot of people we never
get." Persistence gets results in visitation.

6. *Inject Friendliness*

Visitation will certainly be more effective when it
is done in a friendly way. The visitor who displays a
pleasant spirit will soon overcome the suspicion that he
has "an axe to grind." He will be able to warm a cold
heart, open a closed door, and draw out a staid recluse,
by an amiable and gracious manner.

> Friendship ain't just claspin' hands,
>   And saying, "How'de do";
> Friendship grips a feller's heart,
>   And warms him thro' and thro'.

7. *Show Sympathy*

"Finally, be ye all of one mind, having compassion [sympathy] one of another" (1 Peter 3:8). Sympathy is fellow-feeling. It is not so much a verbal expression as it is a kindred spirit and feeling. Sympathy seems to be felt more than heard, yet its effects can certainly be seen.

Being able to enter into the feelings of another is one of the greatest Christian virtues. It finds its highest expression in the ministry of visitation.

8. *Guard Confidences*

The visitor will come to know many confidential matters. He must guard with utmost integrity the things which he observes and hears. It is inexcusable for a visitor to betray confidence in any way.

Unfortunately there are many good people who are indefatigable workers, yet they seemingly cannot refrain from the despicable habit of gossip. The Christian visitor is Christ's ambassador. This lofty position must never be marred by careless tattling, groundless rumor, or idle tales.

III. MAKE PERSONAL PREPARATION

Effective visitation is contingent upon an effective visitor. Preparation is the key to effectiveness. It is no more essential for the Sunday school teacher to be prepared to guide the lesson study than it is for the visitor to be prepared to visit. Preparation must be thorough. All of the visitor's ability, spirit, and personality, as well as much physical strength, is required to do an effective job of visitation.

1. *Present a Pleasing Appearance*

The personal appearance of the visitor is an item of

utmost importance. Certainly he should be neatly, attractively, and appropriately dressed. Such a visitor will make a better impression than one who gives little or no thought to his appearance. The morale of both the visitor and the one to be visited can be greatly improved by the proper attire.

The visitor should remember that he is not on dress parade. It is not necessary to model all of the current fads and fashions. Extreme in costume, as well as an air of expensiveness, ought to be avoided. Naturalness is much more desirable than stylishness.

Generally speaking, men need to guard against being too casual in their appearance. A freshly pressed suit and well-shined shoes will make a great deal of difference in a man's personal appearance. Ladies need to refrain from being ostentatious in their attire. Neatness and appropriateness in dress should characterize the Christian visitor.

2. Have Normal Health

The visitor should be in normal health to do his best work. It is, of course, not advisable to visit when one is ill. However, visitation should not wait on perfect health. Some would never visit since they never seem to feel well! The wise visitor will avoid speaking of his own aches and pains. He will be called upon to listen to the rehearsal of such accomplishments by others!

It is amazing how much better one will feel physically after spending time on the field working for the Lord. There may be a sense of physical fatigue, but the overall physical, emotional, and spiritual lift will more than compensate.

3. Display a Pleasant Personality

A vibrant, Christian personality is a marvelous asset

to the visitor. Christian personality is actually a re-
flection of the personality of Christ. It is grown in
the laboratory of Christian experience and service.

If the visitor's personality does not mirror the
personality of Christ, he will not likely attract others
to Christ.

IV. MAKE MENTAL PREPARATION

There are at least four aspects of mental preparation
necessary before the visitor goes afield for the Lord.

1. Determine the Objective of the Visit

The purpose of the visit must be clearly understood
before a contact is made. Haphazardness is the curse
of visitation. It accomplishes little, if anything. The
visitor must not, as Dr. Robert G. Lee says, "just go to
see folks, nor go to joke or chat, but to do business
for God, to pray, to comfort, to encourage, to win to
Christ, to express joy over work well done."

2. Consider the Individual

The successful visitor must be adroit in the art of
dealing with people. This ability cannot be accomplished without giving considerable time and study to
each individual to be visited. The visitor will need to
recall all he knows about the one to be visited. His
family relations, employment, mutual friends, past
visits, and many other items should be recalled. The
personality type, temperament, emotional response,
and general qualities of the individual are important
items for the visitor to consider.

3. Be Informed

The "know-it-all" is out of place in the field of
Christian visitation, but the visitor should know his

business. He should be able to answer any reasonable questions about the Bible, the church, and the denomination. He should understand the work and program of his own church and have an accurate knowledge of its organizations. Some knowledge of the historical background, present accomplishments, and its future plans would also be valuable to the visitor.

4. *Use the Excuses*

Every visitor sooner or later will encounter many excuses for not attending Sunday school or church. No matter how ridiculous the excuse may be, the visitor must learn how to answer it kindly and courteously. The ability to recognize an excuse and to use it as a clue is indeed a rare accomplishment.

There is a large business concern, specializing in house-to-house selling, which requires its salesmen to memorize the fifty-one stock excuses which women give at their doors. In this way the shrewd salesman is prepared not only to anticipate the excuse and to answer it, but he is also prepared to use the excuse as a valuable part of his sales talk. This is because the excuses and objections given are an indication of the personality type. The discovery of the type is most essential to good salesmanship.

In this connection it would be well for the visitor to know the popular excuses for not attending Sunday school and to be able to use them. The following are offered most frequently. Work out a "sales talk" for each one.

(1) "My parents made me go to church when I was young."

(2) "I have just gotten out of the habit."

(3) "I don't like the preacher (teacher, choir, program, etc.)."

(4) "I have to work six days a week, and Sunday is the only day I have to rest (hunt, fish, wash, etc.)."

(5) "I went there once and no one spoke to me."

(6) "I don't go because the church is always wanting money."

(7) "I know where the church is, and I'll come when I get ready."

(8) "I was brought up in another denomination, and if I went at all, I'd go there."

(9) "I can live just as good a life outside the church as I can in it."

(10) "I may surprise you someday."

V. Make Spiritual Preparation

Visitation is essentially a spiritual ministry. It requires spiritual insight; it demands spiritual perception and spiritual power. A frivolous attitude and a flippant manner seldom produce lasting results. In making spiritual preparation the visitor will:

1. *Pray Before Going*

He should pray for himself, for a realization of the seriousness of his task. He should pray for spiritual strength and foresight. He should pray for a correct attitude and frame of mind. He should pray for wisdom and tact. He should pray for the persons to be visited. He should pray about the purpose of the visit. He should pray about the approach to be made. He should pray that the Holy Spirit will prepare the way and the heart. He should pray that the right Scripture verses may be used. He should pray for the ability to overcome excuses and objections.

Paul's injunction to "pray without ceasing" certainly finds its highest meaning in visitation. The visitor will need to pray before going, during the visit, and afterward that the seed sown may bring fruition in God's own way and time.

2. *Exercise Faith*

The visitor will need to stand firm on the foundation of faith. "According to your faith be it unto you" is as appropriate to the visitor as it was to the blind man in Christ's day. "Only believe" is a divine promise intimating a divine source of power. Too many visitors forget that it requires faith in God to be successful. Too frequently they are reluctant to go. Too often they are fearful of the outcome. These experiences are a sign that one's faith is weak.

Not only will God give strength and the assurance of his presence to the visitor, but he will also give guidance as to what to say. Recall how the Lord stretched forth his hand and touched Jeremiah's mouth while promising to put words in his mouth. God will speak through his servants today if they but exercise faith.

3. *Go in the Strength of the Lord.*

The Christian visitor must never rely upon his own strength or wisdom. This is not only folly, it is unnecessary. The strength of the Almighty is available. God's promise to Joshua is valid today, "Be strong and of a good courage; be not afraid, neither be thou dismayed: for the Lord thy God is with thee whithersoever thou goest" (Josh. 1: 9).

FOR CLASS DISCUSSION

Based on this chapter, you may wish to prepare a self-rating chart for visitors, and then let each class member use it (privately) to evaluate himself.

CHAPTER 5

I. Learn to Make Impressive Contacts
   1. Time the Visit Effectively
   2. Make the Proper Approach
   3. Win a Hearing

II. Guide the Conversation
   1. "Warm Up" the Prospect
   2. Make the Transition
   3. Present the Proposition
   4. Make the Appeal
   5. Secure the Commitment

III. Make a Graceful Exit
   1. Do Not "Shake Off the Dust"
   2. Do Not Give Up

IV. Check the Results

V

Mastering the Art of Visitation

VISITATION is the finest of the fine arts. Mastering such an art requires a lifetime of careful effort. Training is important; study is essential. The visitor who seeks to gain the mastery of this art must give unceasing attention to details. Only constant practice, an indefatigable spirit, and a compassionate heart will ever guarantee success.

In the final analysis, successful visitation is a personal accomplishment gained only by painstaking effort. This does not mean that the inexperienced visitor cannot do good work. It merely emphasizes the fact that mastery of the visitation art is a long and tedious climb worth every effort it demands.

I. LEARN TO MAKE IMPRESSIVE CONTACTS

Although the ability to make an impressive contact is not often a gift, it can be readily developed. It requires thinking in terms of the person to be visited. The most impressive contacts will be made by those who are able to visualize themselves in the other person's place. The visitor who does this will:

1. *Time the Visit Effectively*

The wise visitor will not call at an inappropriate time. Such a procedure will not gain the attention of the prospect. Poor timing may cause embarrassment or even resentment on the part of the person being visited. When a visitor finds that he has chosen an inopportune time, he should excuse himself graciously, and, if possible, make an appointment.

Often a visit is delayed until it is ineffective. This is particularly true in cases of illness or distress. For example, those who are bereaved should be visited immediately, but they should not be neglected after the funeral service.

On the other hand, a visit can be made too soon, as in the case of surgery.

In timing the visit, one should choose the time that meets the need of the one to be visited.

2. *Make the Proper Approach*

The visitor should remember that first impressions are lasting impressions. His approach may open or close the door of opportunity. The visitor who recognizes this fact will:

(1) *Extend a hearty greeting.*—The friendly, decorous handclasp of a man who is glad to see another man —the kindly, gracious greeting of a lovely Christian woman delighted to see another woman—these constitute a hearty greeting. Such a greeting is felt more than spoken.

(2) *Wear a sincere smile.*—An "east-to-west" smile —all over the face—is intriguing. Of course, it must not be overdone; rather it should be warm and natural. A smiling face is lovely to look upon even though it

might not be classed as a masterpiece of beauty. The Christian visitor must remember that a smile is "worth a million dollars, but it doesn't cost a cent."

(3) *Stand "tall."*—A shuffling, slumping figure is certainly not conducive to an effective approach. One may be casual without coming apart at the joints. An erect and buoyant posture not only helps one approach his prospect more efficiently, but it also is a boon to the visitor's morale.

(4) *Use pleasing voice tones.*—A whining or mumbling visitor is the "abomination of desolation standing where it ought not." Cordiality, sincerity, and enthusiasm are quickly discerned in the voice tones. Words too softly spoken are unintelligible, yet one must remember that speaking too loudly is repulsive.

(5) *Enunciate carefully.*—The visitor must be sure that he speaks clearly and distinctly. It is of utmost importance that his name be understood as well as the name of the church he represents. It is foolish to give a "sales talk" if it cannot be easily understood. The visitor must watch not only his pronunciation, but also the speed of his talking. Talking too slowly or too rapidly will guarantee a poor and ineffective conversation.

(6) *Be mentally alert.*—Securing a quick grasp of the situation is dependent upon staying awake mentally. Common experiences which serve as clues for guiding the conversation should be noted. Opportunities for further service should be observed.

(7) *Radiate confidence.*—The good visitor will have an air of confidence which comes from being properly prepared for his visit and from being thoroughly sold on his mission. His confidence will be further enhanced by the knowledge that he is serving God in exactly the

same way that Jesus served. Such confidence will help the visitor to "endure hardness, as a good soldier of Jesus Christ" (2 Tim. 2:3). It will fortify him against embarrassment, insult, indifference, or discourtesy. It will help him endure patiently and joyfully any unsatisfactory experiences. "And they departed from the presence of the council, rejoicing that they were counted worthy to suffer shame for his name" (Acts 5:41).

3. *Win a Hearing*

Getting one's foot in the door may offset having the door shut in one's face, but it can also be painful to bunions! High-pressure methods in visitation are not in keeping with the spirit of Christianity. However, winning a hearing is another matter. It is essential to successful visitation.

It is rather axiomatic that no individual can be won to a new loyalty without first being won to the person who is attempting to influence him. "And ye became followers of us, and of the Lord, having received the word" (1 Thess. 1:6). The visitor must remember that those whom he seeks to win must first be won to confidence in the visitor himself. Breaking down the barriers is prerequisite to making visitation operative. The following suggestions have been found helpful in winning a hearing:

(1) *Use the individual's name.*—It has been said that the sweetest word in the English language is one's own name. The wise visitor will obtain the name of the individual to be visited and will use it discreetly and frequently in the conversation. This not only makes it easier to win a hearing, but it also simplifies remembering the name.

(2) *Make appropriate introductions.*—Most people are wary of a stranger. The visitor will, therefore, introduce himself at once. Even though the visitor's name may not mean anything to the person being visited, the fact that he is willing to give his name means much. It is also wise to mention the name of the church in which the visitor holds membership and to present the official calling card of the church. It is often a good policy, especially for men, to indicate one's business connections as a matter of identification. If there are other visitors in the party, they, too, should be properly and carefully introduced.

(3) *Ask to be admitted.*—If the visitor is not invited into the house and there seems to be no reason for closing the visit, it is not at all out of order to ask to be admitted. Of course, the request should be tactfully made. Asking to be admitted is often necessary because of the natural reserve of many good people. This is especially true of those persons who have not been called upon before by a church visitor. It is a new experience to them.

It must be remembered that people are visited so infrequently in the interest of a church they are often at a loss as to what to say. This should not cause any serious concern on the part of a consecrated visitor. A simple request, "May I come in?" is all that will be necessary in most cases. A repeat visit may be necessary before gaining entrance, but a wise visitor will eventually get inside with his message.

There are certain circumstances under which the visitor should not seek admittance. He will be able to sense these occasions readily. A friendly greeting and a promise to come again at a more convenient time will almost guarantee an audience later.

II. GUIDE THE CONVERSATION

Securing admission into the home is not the end. It is only the beginning. What turn shall the conversation take? How may the major purpose of the visit be approached. The person visited may be apprehensive, perhaps even defensive. He may not be ready for any proposition. He may be coldly indifferent.

1. *"Warm Up" the Prospect*

It would be folly to approach the purpose of the visit immediately. The groundwork must be laid. An indifferent prospect must be "warmed up." How?

(1) *Get him to talk.*—Nothing will "warm up" a person more than hearing his own voice. If he is not inclined to talk, ask questions. The most successful questions will be those which are directed toward the personal interests of the person visited. Questions about the family, employment, hobbies, and mutual friends are excellent conversation starters. Often an object in the room will indicate a special interest which may be the magic key to the prospect's heart.

(2) *Show a personal interest in the prospect.*—If the visitor is to gain a hearing, he must not only get the person to talk, but he must also show a personal interest in what is being said. Disraeli said: "Talk to a man about himself, and he will listen for hours."

(3) *Make the person feel worth while.*—A good visitor will find a way to make the one being visited feel that he is appreciated. This does not call for, nor even suggest, hypocrisy or flattery. Insincerity is a sin that can be easily detected, but an expression of appreciation is such a simple thing that it is a sin not to make it.

2. *Make the Transition*

Up to this point the conversation, though probably very interesting, has been of an incidental nature. It is time to move on to the major objective of the visit. If the visitor has a well-defined purpose in mind, he will be more successful in changing the conversation from the personal to the spiritual.

(1) *Change smoothly.*—The transition from the personal to the spiritual should come smoothly and gradually. To change the subject abruptly defeats the purpose of the "warm-up" period.

(2) *Change naturally.*—It is often good to use "tie-on" statements in making the transition. It is quite natural to say: "That reminds me of . . . ," or, "Another interesting thing about that is . . . ," or, "There is a question I want to ask you. . . ."

It has also been found quite natural to use a story or illustration to lead up to one's objective. This is most helpful in keeping the interest of the prospect and in bringing it to the focal point. Jesus was so expert in this respect that it is difficult to determine the exact place where he turned the conversation to the spiritual needs.

3. *Present the Proposition*

The moment has arrived for which the visit was made. The visitor must keep in mind his purpose and proceed in a logical and practical manner to reach the objective. The skill with which he guides the discussion will largely determine his success. The procedure will be determined by the nature of the visit. Special types of visitation will be considered later in this book, so only general suggestions are given here:

(1) Follow a simple step-by-step presentation, taking time to be sure the prospect understands.

(2) Use the Scriptures to support the propositions.

(3) Anticipate and answer as many questions and problems as possible.

(4) Avoid any arguments. Do not raise the voice.

(5) Depend upon the Holy Spirit.

When more than one person is in the visiting party, it is best that one person do most of the talking. There is a tendency to digress when others assist too freely. This tendency is one of the reasons for keeping the visiting party small. One or two members is ample in most cases.

4. *Make the Appeal*

When the visitor has reached the climax of his proposition, he should watch carefully for the best time to make the appeal. This is the time to be careful about digression. Regardless of the nature of the appeal, it is essential that the issue be kept close to the heart of the prospect.

Earnestness on the part of the visitor is most important. Prayer is frequently in order. Scripture reading will help. A word of testimony from the other member of the visiting team will often be the right thing. No pressure is to be used, for this is a spiritual appeal and things of the Spirit cannot be forced.

5. *Secure the Commitment*

This is the most delicate part of the visit. It means the difference between success and failure.

(1) *Watch for the right time.*—Do not ask for a verdict until the opportune moment has come. When the Holy Spirit begins to strive, yielding time has come. Show the need of an immediate settlement of the issue. Indicate the folly of neglect, but do not preach. Appeal, but do not exhort.

(2) *Avoid a negative answer.*—Lead up to the commitment by asking a question or two that must be answered positively. Let the prospect get in the habit of saying yes. Help him feel the urgency for immediate decision. Do not rush or overpersuade, for this can do much harm at this point.

If the prospect shows clearly that he is going to make the wrong decision, do not press for answer that will commit him to the wrong choice. It would be better for him to say nothing than to say no.

(3) *Do not give up.*—When the best policy seems to be to wait for a later commitment, do not give up in defeat. Let the individual feel that the matter has not been settled, and urge him to make the right choice. Recommend his careful consideration. Leave him something to read on the subject and promise to return after he has had more time to consider the matter.

III. MAKE A GRACEFUL EXIT

A friendly departure will leave the door open for a return visit. So, in leaving a home, no matter what the circumstances, do not slam the door! Leave it open! Many victories can be won for Christ simply by showing a Christlike attitude when leaving.

1. *Do Not "Shake Off the Dust"*

It is easy to decide that there is little use in returning to any given home. A Christian visitor must never lose control of himself to such an extent that he declares he shall not visit any particular person again. He should display the spirit of the Master who sought unceasingly until he found the sheep that was lost (Luke 15).

2. *Do Not Give Up*

The patient, persistent visitor is the successful one. There is never a time to give up in visitation. One young man enrolled in a Sunday school class and came under conviction of sin. He dropped out of the class, but the members began to visit him. Every time they called, he made it a point to be in the bathtub. This happened so often that it became a joke among those who visited him.

The teacher and the faithful members did not give up even in the face of this discouragement. They continued to visit the young man regularly for eight years. He was eventually won to Christ and church membership as a result of the faithful class in visitation.

IV. CHECK THE RESULTS

Even though the visitor may reasonably expect to make many visits to any given individual, it is well to keep in mind that each visit may be the last one the prospect will ever have. This means that every visit must be effective and profitable. How can the visitor be assured of doing his best work?

Each visit could be profitably studied in the light of the following evaluation:

1. Did I time my visit properly?
2. Did I gain a cordial hearing?
3. Was my approach effective?
4. Did I present my proposition intelligently?
5. Was my appeal convincing?
6. Did I depend upon the Holy Spirit?
7. Did I gain my objective?
8. Am I welcome to return soon?
9. When shall I call again?
10. How may I make a better approach?

A prayerful evaluation of the visit will reveal points of strength and of weakness. The visitor should plan how the next visit can be used to overcome or offset the weak points. But remember, the visit that is prompted by love and that is in the Master's name, under the guidance of the Holy Spirit does produce results.

FOR CLASS DISCUSSION

At the close of the study of this chapter, list the ideas you have gained that will enable you to be a better visitor from now on.

CHAPTER 6

I. DEVELOP A DESIRE FOR ENLARGEMENT
  1. A Desire to Reach More People Springs from a Compassionate Heart
  2. It Depends upon an Enlarged Vision
  3. It Stems from Wise Leadership

II. WORK THROUGH THE CLASS ORGANIZATION
  1. The President Must Lead in Class Visitation
  2. The Group Leader Must Co-operate in Visitation
  3. The Vice-president Creates a Warm Fellowship Through Visitation
  4. The Secretary Provides Incentives for Visitation

III. USE THE DEPARTMENT ORGANIZATION
  1. The Officers Work Together
  2. The Classes Co-operate
  3. The Members Assist

IV. PREVENT ABSENTEEISM
  1. The Proper Procedure for Enrolling New Members Must Be Followed
  2. The Legitimate Reasons for Dropping Names Must Be Known
  3. Better Teaching Must Be Seen as the Key to the Prevention of Absenteeism

V. REACH THE LAST PERSON
  1. Age Grading Is the Basis
  2. Annual Promotion Assists
  3. The Cradle Roll Reaches the Babies
  4. The Extension Department Provides for Those Who Cannot Attend

VI

Visiting to Enlarge the Sunday School

And the lord said unto the servant, Go out into the highways and hedges, and compel them to come in, that my house may be filled. Luke 14:23

GROWING a great Sunday school is unquestionably one of the most effective ways of reaching people with the gospel message. This fact is causing many churches to give serious attention to creating an efficient Sunday school organization. The wisdom of this policy is shown by the fact that these churches are reaching large numbers for Christ. Many churches are now winning several hundred to Christ each year simply by utilizing the Sunday school in the visitation program of the church.

J. N. Barnette—lovingly called "Mr. Sunday School" by Southern Baptists—has said: "Visitation is the chief factor in Sunday school growth, the final step is actually reaching people. A Sunday school may have adequate space, properly arranged, a sufficient number of classes, excellent teaching, attractive programs, and how vitally essential they are; but the one thing without which all these will be at least a partial failure is visitation."

In the final analysis there is really only one way to enlarge a Sunday school and to keep its members attending regularly. This is accomplished only through a continuous, systematic visitation program. This is as true in the rural area as in the city. It is as true in the village as in the town. Each Sunday school will face some local problems in its schedule. There will also be some details of transportation to be worked out in each community; however, the basic principles of visitation are the same in every locality.

Effective use of the Sunday school in visitation is not an accident. It must be carefully planned, properly motivated, and persistently promoted if the best results are to be secured.

I. DEVELOP A DESIRE FOR ENLARGEMENT

It may seem trite to say that "every Sunday school should grow," yet there are many that are not increasing their attendance. Decreasing attendances, loss of interest, falling enrolments, and failing morale are indications of spiritual distress. These churches need to become more conscious of the people they are failing to reach.

1. *A Desire to Reach More People Springs from a Compassionate Heart*

Every Christian possessing any degree of compassion has a deep-seated desire to reach more people for Christ. This intense desire has occasionally been misunderstood. Some have called it a craze for numbers. There may be sincerity behind such a statement, but more than likely it is an unconscious attempt to rationalize one's own failure. Regardless of the reason, such an attitude is unwholesome.

The desire to reach more people is more than a craze for numbers; it is a passion for souls! Every right-thinking person knows that it is always the will of the Father to reach more souls with the gospel. It is a truism that the first test of the Sunday school is the numbers test. The real test is likewise not how many have been reached but how many are still unreached.

2. *It Depends upon an Enlarged Vision*

Solomon wrote: "Where there is no vision, the people perish" (Prov. 29:18). The compelling urge to reach more people springs from the fountain of spiritual vision. It is the vision of a lost world that urges one to visit. It is a vision of the vast multitudes without Christ that arouses a church from its lethargy and sends its members out into the white harvest fields. It is a vision of the unreached masses that turns a Sunday school's halfhearted efforts into a mighty rushing stream sweeping the multitudes into its organization for teaching and soul-winning. It is a vision of the tragic condition of a lost soul that causes the Sunday school worker to leave his pleasurable pursuits to search the paths of sin for a wandering pupil. It is an enlarged vision which magnifies the urgency for enlarging the Sunday school.

3. *It Stems from Wise Leadership*

Some leaders who lack spiritual insight have resorted to cheap promotional stunts to increase the Sunday school attendance. Some have sought to lure the people by providing a constant parade of visiting dignitaries. Others have resorted to entertainment and clubroom methods. Contests of every type have been tried so often that many of the members see "red" and have the "blues." Prizes, bribes, and other claptrap methods have been pawned off on the people, but the plain truth is that they will not consistently attend for such trivial reasons.

The Lord's people must learn that the Lord's business must be done in the Lord's way. Visitation is the only answer to consistent Sunday school growth. Wise leaders are aware of this fact and seek to create a desire for enlargement by helping their workers to understand their opportunities. They make use of attendance goals. They use slogans, mottoes, songs, and other media for keeping the people aware of their opportunities. They review the accomplishments of other schools; they check on their own past achievements. They seek to keep their workers close to the compassionate heart of the Lord, for that is the very source of the desire to reach others.

II. WORK THROUGH THE CLASS ORGANIZATION

Every Sunday school worker should visit. However, the officers and teachers alone cannot reach large numbers of people. This does not excuse them from their responsibility, but it emphasizes the fact that they need and deserve the assistance of their class members.

The teacher will, of course, bear the burden of the class, but the members of older classes are as obligated before God to visit as the teacher. It is not a matter of time nor inclination for the class member, since the commission "to go" rests upon every Christian. Each class member should share in the work of visitation if the class is to discharge its obligation to the people.

The genius of the class organization shows up best in the matter of visitation. Reaching people is the major function of the class organization. Consider briefly how each class officer is delegated some of the responsibility of visitation.

1. *The President Must Lead in Class Visitation*

Along with his duties as presiding officer, the president is charged with building the class spirit for reaching people. He will co-operate with the superintendent of enlargement and lead the class in its visitation work. Since the major task of the class is reaching people, he is responsible to see that the class performs its duty in seeking to enlist all the prospects within the age range assigned to the class. He will work with the group leaders charged with enlisting prospects and reclaiming the absentees.

The president is also responsible for leading the class to attain and maintain the Standard of Excellence which provides for class enlargement through visitation:

"(1) The class shall promote a program of visitation. All members shall be visited during the year.
"(2) All accessible absentees and newly enrolled members shall be communicated with during the following week.
"(3) The class shall co-operate with the department and school in all enlargement efforts."

2. *The Group Leader Must Co-operate in Visitation*

The group leader is a vital assistant in the field of enlargement and is directly responsible for helping build a group spirit for reaching people. Under the direction of the class president and the superintendent of enlargement he will co-operate in all enlargement activities. He will seek to build the attendance and to enlarge the class through hearty participation in the weekly visitation program.

3. *The Vice-president Creates a Warm Fellowship Through Visitation*

The primary task of the vice-president is to make the class attractive to the members and prospective members. It will be impossible to know the members well enough to accomplish this assignment unless considerable visitation is done. Creating a warm-hearted fellowship logically demands a large amount of warmhearted visitation.

4. *The Secretary Provides Incentives for Visitation*

The secretary and his records will provide incentives for the visitation work of the class. His records will reveal the particular needs of each member. Although the secretary's major task is to keep the other officers informed, he will also assist in the work of visitation as an aid to his own spiritual development. A class secretary can accomplish much with the appropriate and discreet use of his class records.

III. Use the Department Organization

Department Sunday schools will find the department organization most helpful in promoting a sensible visitation program. The purpose of the department organization is the correlation of the work of its classes. This is most effective in projecting the visitation program.

1. *The Officers Work Together*

The department school will require an officer in charge of visitation in each department. This officer will be in charge of all phases of enlargement and will direct the visitation program of the department. He will work in close co-operation with the superintendent of enlargement who has general oversight of the enlargement of the entire Sunday school. He will also work closely with the class presidents and group leaders.

2. *The Classes Co-operate*

Since the department seeks to work in full harmony with the general Sunday school visitation policy, it will be necessary for the classes to co-operate with the department efforts in visitation. This means that the class officers will work with the department associate superintendent. They will project a program that will bring the best results both for the department and the classes.

3. *The Members Assist*

The co-operation of the departments in the visitation program offers an unusual opportunity for utilizing all the class members. The hearty assistance of each class member greatly enhances the effectiveness of the visitation program and guarantees an ever-enlarging Sunday school.

IV. PREVENT ABSENTEEISM

Sunday school enlargement is much more than reaching new members. It is entirely possible for a Sunday school to have a constant stream of new members and yet fail to grow. Holding those who have already been reached is essential to Sunday school enlargement. Probably the key to enlargement is as much a matter of preventing absenteeism as it is a matter of enlisting new members.

1. *The Proper Procedure for Enrolling New Members Must Be Followed*

When should a pupil be enrolled? Just as soon as he so desires, the very first Sunday if possible. This is best both for the pupil and for the teacher because it creates a sense of belonging for the pupil and a sense of certain responsibility for the teacher. The Sunday school exists for the good of the pupil, and there should be no restrictions for membership in the school.

The proper procedure for enrolling new members would in most cases alleviate a great part of the absentee problem. This procedure may be outlined as follows:

(1) It should be made clear to the pupil that he is joining the Sunday school rather than a class. (Having a general classification officer to supervise the enrolment of all new members and secure the necessary information is vital.)

(2) He should be placed in a class according to his classification age.

(3) He should be assigned to a group and introduced to his group leader. Group assignment does not apply to children below Junior age.

(4) He should receive a warm welcome from the members of the class.

(5) He should be supplied with proper lesson helps.

(6) He should receive an explanation of the record system.

(7) He should be visited by the teacher during the following week. The teacher will assure the pupil of his earnest desire to be of spiritual service. He will seek to weld the bond of friendship that has been formed. The wise teacher will remember that the new member has not yet formed the habit of Sunday school attendance and will provide opportunities to make his regular attendance meaningful.

2. *The Legitimate Reasons for Dropping Names Must Be Known*

Some Sunday school workers have attempted to wash their hands of responsibility by dropping all members who fail to attend for three or four Sundays. Such a practice is incongruous with the purpose of the Sunday school. The pupils who are attending do not need the class as much as those who are not attending. Actually there are only three reasons for dropping a name:

(1) The pupil moves away.
(2) The pupil transfers to another Sunday school.
(3) The pupil dies.

Someone has said that the only way for a pupil to get off the class roll is for him to "die off, move off, or run off."

3. *Better Teaching Must Be Seen as the Key to the Prevention of Absenteeism*

The real key to the problem of absenteeism and its prevention lies at the door of the teacher. It is possible to get almost anyone to attend Sunday school once or twice, but the habit of regular attendance rests almost entirely upon the teacher rather than the pupil.

The pupil must feel that he is getting something that makes his attendance worth while. This means that the teacher must teach pupils, not lessons; that he must meet spiritual needs, not cover a lesson; that he must teach creatively, not transmissively.

A teacher has two great concerns: to faithfully teach the revealed Word of God, and to do it with the pupils' growth and development as a central purpose. Any teacher who is willing to pay the price for improvement in teaching will also reap the dividend of sustained attendance on the part of his pupils.

V. REACH THE LAST PERSON

This is much more than an idealistic dream. It is a glorious possibility. It is also a proof of the divine wisdom of God in providing a method that could reach the very last individual in any given community. His method for reaching people is well able to reach to the farthest outpost. It is possible for Christian people to reach the very last person with the gospel simply through the medium of personal visitation. This can be done by using all of the church agencies, but the Sunday school plays a peculiarly important role.

1. *Age Grading Is the Basis*

Age grading, or class formation by age, is the only known method of grading that can logically make everyone in the community the responsibility of someone in the church. The fixing of such responsibility is enough to commend this practice, but beyond this a teacher of any given age group is relieved of any definite responsibility for enlisting those outside his class range.

2. *Annual Promotion Assists*

Age grading alone will not keep the ideal of reaching the last person in the realm of possibility. Annual promotion must be observed to keep a school properly graded. This is as important in Young People's and Adult classes as in the younger departments. It is only in this way that age grading can guarantee the enlistment possibilities of the Sunday school.

3. *The Cradle Roll Reaches the Babies*

Reaching the last person demands that some provision be made for the babies who do not attend on Sunday morning. In fact a good portion of the Sunday school growth depends upon their being reached. Since the work of the Cradle Roll is essentially a visitation ministry, it becomes a constant source of Sunday school enlargement, placing both children and adults in the membership. By providing a home ministry the Cradle Roll department gains an entrance into many homes that otherwise would be closed to the Sunday school.

4. *The Extension Department Provides for Those Who Cannot Attend*

It would be impossible to reach the last person in the community apart from a functioning Extension department. This is because a sizable percentage of the population simply cannot attend Sunday school due to employment, poor health, and other unavoidable hindrances. The Extension department not only brings Bible study to these neglected persons, but it also makes possible Sunday school enlargement in a most practical way.

FOR CLASS DISCUSSION

Face up honestly to the work of your class and your department, and seek to decide how you can make it function more effectively in Sunday school enlargement through visitation.

CHAPTER 7

I. VISITATION HELPS THE TEACHER UNDERSTAND THE PUPIL
   1. It Reveals the Influences of the Home
   2. It Gives an Insight into the Religious Background
   3. It Aids in Discovering Personal Needs

II. VISITATION HELPS THE PUPIL UNDERSTAND THE TEACHER
   1. It Alleviates Personality Barriers
   2. It Provides Opportunity for a Growing Friendship

III. VISITATION HELPS THE TEACHER SECURE HOME CO-OPERATION
   1. It Establishes Confidence in the Teacher
   2. It Enlists the Home as an Ally

IV. VISITATION HELPS THE TEACHER PLAN HIS TEACHING
   1. It Simplifies the Formulation of the Lesson Aim
   2. It Facilitates an Interesting Beginning
   3. It Insures the Choice of Right Methods
   4. It Stimulates Appropriate Illustrations

V. VISITATION HELPS THE TEACHER MAKE HIS TEACHING PRACTICAL

VI. VISITATION HELPS THE TEACHER TEST HIS TEACHING

VII

Visiting to Improve Teaching

VISITATION is uniquely related to the teaching task. Too few teachers seem to realize this fact. Many view visitation chiefly as a means of securing better attendance on the part of their pupils. This type of visitation is definitely essential. Very little can be done for the pupil who does not attend. Yet, as far as the teacher is concerned, there is a much more important reason for visiting. It is to improve the quality of his teaching.

I. VISITATION HELPS THE TEACHER UNDERSTAND THE PUPIL

Someone has wisely said, "No teacher can do his best work in the classroom if his knowledge of the pupil is limited to the classroom." The more the teacher learns about his pupils, the more effective will be his teaching.

It is not sufficient that the teacher know his pupils or class in general; he must know the individual in a specific manner. It is, of course, much easier for a teacher to come to know the individual pupil when he knows and understands the psychology of his particular age group.

The general physical, mental, spiritual, and social traits of the particular group should be thoroughly understood, but the individual differences are more important than the similarities. The teacher must know and appreciate each pupil's qualities so well that each one can be given individual attention. When the teacher has acquired this skill, each pupil will leave the classroom feeling that the lesson was meant for him.

1. *It Reveals the Influences of the Home*

Every teacher should strive to know as much about each pupil as the other members in the home know. The teacher will need to know how many are in the family, their approximate ages, and their interests. He will be concerned with all the problems in the home.

The teacher will need information about the family activities in the social realm. He will be interested in the religious life of the family, whether or not family worship is held, blessing said at mealtime, etc. The teacher will tactfully acquaint himself with the economic status of the family. He will recognize the emotional condition of the family as an item of vital importance. He will be keenly interested in the relation of the home to the local community.

2. *It Gives an Insight into the Religious Background*

It is most important that the teacher have detailed information about the pupil's religious background and experience. If the pupil is above the age of accountability, then the teacher must be sure about the conversion experience. This is the most serious and far-reaching responsibility of the teacher.

The matter of the pupil's church membership should be of concern to the teacher. Other matters, such as the regularity of Sunday school attendance, attendance upon the worship services, and other church organizational meetings, are essential information.

The personal habits of the Christian life should be studied. Does the pupil engage in daily Bible reading, meditation, and prayer? Does he possess good factual knowledge of the Bible? Will he pray in public? Has he strong moral and spiritual convictions? Does he have at least a basic understanding of the doctrines?

The pupil's response and fidelity to the class and its functions are important. Does he participate in the lesson study? Does he visit and assist with the class activities? Is he a soul-winner? All of these are of the greatest significance to the teacher.

3. It Aids in Discovering Personal Needs

Only the teacher's careful study of each class member will enable him to understand the problems and difficulties of their lives. A knowledge of these things is essential if the teacher is to bring the necessary emphasis that will aid the pupil in correcting and solving his problems.

The problems of a spiritual nature are of paramount concern to the teacher. They are followed closely by the moral and social, and are interrelated. The sincere teacher will take note of the weakness and virtues of the pupil. He will consider prejudices, peevishness, and depths of feeling that the pupil displays. He will explore the realm of pupil attitudes, aptitudes, and abilities. He will discover interests, hobbies, reading habits, and type of companions, and will relate these to pupil needs.

When the teacher secures this wide scope of information about his pupils, he is in a position to be of real service as he seeks to point the pupil to "a more excellent way." Such information cannot be gained unless the teacher spends time in close association with the pupil. It will require frequent visitation and close observation.

This information is too valuable to the teacher for him to seek to retain it all in his mind. There must be a way to record it and preserve it for study. The wise teacher studies his class records as closely as he studies the lesson materials.

Various methods are used to preserve the information about each pupil. Mimeographed sheets which have been devised to fit the needs of a particular age group are used by many teachers. An excellent teacher's record book designed for each age group is published by the Baptist Sunday School Board, Nashville, Tennessee.

II. Visitation Helps the Pupil Understand the Teacher

The teaching-learning process is a twofold effort. It is just as important that the pupil understand the teacher as it is for the teacher to understand the pupil. Visitation is the master key which unlocks both the teacher-heart and the pupil-heart.

1. *It Alleviates Personality Barriers*

There is a certain comradeship necessary between the teacher and pupil before the most effective teaching-learning can take place. Oftentimes there are differences in personality which handicap learning. These differences must be understood. There may be difficult reservations that need to be broken down. The pupil must know that the teacher's interest is genuine and that it is motivated by the desire to be helpful.

2. *It Provides Opportunity for a Growing Friendship*

The ideal relationship between teacher and pupil cannot be gained overnight. Intimate friendships come only between those who spend much time together. The sharing of thoughts, ambitions, and desires will enter into the matter. Experiences, investigations, and mutual participation in various activities help weld two personalities into a meaningful friendship.

III. VISITATION HELPS THE TEACHER SECURE HOME CO-OPERATION

The deep significance of the relationship between the home and the church is being more fully realized. The home and the church are the only institutions which God has established. They are inseparably related. The attitude of one toward the other has a far-reaching effect.

As the teacher visits in the home, he realizes that the effectiveness of his teaching is largely dependent upon the response of the home. The radio, movies, television, magazines, and many other things exert a powerful influence over the pupil, but nothing quite compares with the impact of the home. Regardless of the age of the pupil, the teacher's major concern will be the reaction of the home to his teaching.

1. *It Establishes Confidence in the Teacher*

As the teacher enters the home, his attitude must be one of friendliness. He should seek to bring an inspiration to the home. He should make his contacts with a view toward encouraging those in the home.

Taking a spirit of joy into the home will make the teacher a welcome guest at any time. The wise teacher will plan for his visit to create a pleasurable break in the home routine. This kind of visitation will do much to win the home, thereby making the winning of the pupil much easier.

2. *It Enlists the Home as an Ally*

The teacher who has won the confidence of the family can more readily enlist the home as an ally. He will be in a better position to engage in tactful efforts to eliminate the competitive aspects in many homes. Regular attendance at Sunday school and preaching services can be obtained when the teacher takes the time to explain its value.

Bible study can be secured when the home is enlisted to promote it. The Six Point Record System will be looked upon as a character building instrument when it is discussed in the home. There are few problems which cannot either be completely solved or greatly helped by a sensible approach through visitation.

IV. VISITATION HELPS THE TEACHER PLAN HIS TEACHING

Teaching is chiefly concerned with helping one's pupils work out their spiritual problems. It is essential, therefore, that the teacher consider these problems in his teaching plan. This means that his lesson plan will be greatly influenced by his visitation. Visitation will exert a crystallizing effect upon his thinking as he plans the lesson procedure.

1. *It Simplifies the Formulation of the Lesson Aim*

When the time comes to determine the lesson aim, the teacher will need to recall his visitation experiences. This will enable him to decide what information, inspiration, attitudes, appreciations, skills, and changes in conduct his pupils will need to gain from the lesson. It is in this way that visitation assists in formulating a clearly defined aim.

2. *It Facilitates an Interesting Beginning*

The point of contact must be concerned with the pupil's interests and be centered in life. The teacher who has been in close contact with his pupils will know immediately which story, question, object, or statement will be needed to capture the interest of his pupils.

The attention getter may be an incident or experience gained through visitation. It may be a reference to a more or less personal matter which is pertinent to the lesson. It may be an opinion expressed by some class member or other person during a visit. Probably the most interesting points of contact are found through visitation.

3. *It Insures the Choice of Right Methods*

The main difference between an interesting lesson and one which is boring is the method of presentation. The teacher who enjoys a close association with his pupils will know how each pupil responds and can adapt his methods accordingly. He will select the methods that are best suited to meeting the specific needs of the pupils. This means that the methods will vary throughout the class period as pupil and truth are drawn closer together. The dull, dry, drab lesson is a sure sign of a nonvisiting teacher.

4. *It Stimulates Appropriate Illustrations*

Interesting and helpful illustrations are readily available to the teacher who visits. The homes which he contacts are marked by struggle and failure, success and tragedy, comedy and chagrin, which illustrate Bible truths. A wise teacher will never be guilty of betraying a confidence or reflecting unfavorably upon any home.   Rather, he will make use of life experiences to drive home a point without bruising a heart.

V. Visitation Helps the Teacher Make His Teaching Practical

The teacher who fails to visit will be tempted to feel that he has discharged his teaching obligation with the presentation of the lesson facts.   He will not recognize that his obligation includes a practical demonstration of the lesson by the pupils in their daily lives.

The most practical teaching is that which is related to, and centered in, life.   The teacher who does not visit will be hindered in interpreting the daily experiences of his pupils.   He will miss many opportunities for personal counseling.   He will be handicapped in guiding his pupils in their spiritual growth and development.   He will not be too successful in channeling the talents of his class members into Christian service. In short, his teaching will be more factual than it will be practical.

VI. Visitation Helps the Teacher Test His Teaching

Sunday school teachers are often perplexed as to the effectiveness of their teaching.   Various methods for testing teaching have been devised, yet the real test is the daily life of the pupil.   It is not so much what a pupil says, but what he does that reveals the merits of the teacher.

The full extent of the pupil's improvement can be measured by his conduct in the home, the school, the shop, the store, and on the street rather than in the classroom.   It is through frequent association with the pupil that the teacher may observe the results of his work.

In the final analysis, visitation is the mirror in which the teacher's success or failure is clearly reflected.

FOR CLASS DISCUSSION

Some of you are teachers. This chapter speaks right to you. No doubt your main response will be earnest prayer for guidance and impowering in your visitation ministry.

Others who study this book are not teachers. Will you resolve (1) to pray for the teachers in your Sunday school as they visit and (2) to carry the load of visitation to absentees and prospects so that your teacher can concentrate on other objectives in his visitation?

CHAPTER 8

I. RECOGNIZE THE OPPORTUNITIES FOR VISITATION-EVANGE-LISM

1. The Unsaved Class Members Take Priority
2. Many Relatives of the Sunday School Members Are Lost
3. The Parents of the Cradle Roll Babies Need to Be Won
4. The Members of the Extension Department Must Be Evangelized
5. The Vacation Bible School Registration Cards Reveal Evangelistic Opportunities

II. UNDERSTAND THE REQUIREMENTS FOR VISITATION-EVANGE-LISM

1. The Visitor Should Know That He Is Genuinely Born Again
2. The Visitor Must Understand His Responsibility Toward the Lost
3. The Visitor Must Realize What It Means to Be Lost
4. The Visitor Must Know the Plan of Salvation
5. The Visitor Should Understand the Problems to Be Solved

III. FOLLOW THE MASTER'S PROCEDURE IN VISITATION-EVANGE-LISM

1. Make a Tactful Approach
2. Create a Deeper Interest
3. Produce a Sense of Conviction
4. Correct a Misunderstanding
5. Reveal the Way of Salvation
6. Secure an Open Confession
7. Instruct the New Convert

IV. USE THE SCRIPTURES IN VISITATION-EVANGELISM

1. Read the Bible Rather than Quote It
2. Make the Scripture Message Personal
3. Mark Certain Verses for the Unsaved

VIII

Visiting to Win the Lost

And they that be wise shall shine as the brightness of the firmament; and they that turn many to righteousness as the stars for ever and ever. Daniel 12:3

THE most convincing argument for a thorough program of visitation lies in the matchless opportunities it affords for soul-winning. This accounts for the prevailing emphasis on visitation-evangelism. It is not a new method but simply a practical application of the basic procedure which Christ used. In the home, as in no other place, the visitor will enjoy presenting the claims of Christ in a personal, heart-searching manner.

I. Recognize the Opportunities for Visitation-Evangelism

As much as 85 per cent of all the professions of faith in most Southern Baptist churches comes directly through the Sunday school. This fact indicates that the greatest evangelistic opportunities are found within the homes of those who are connected in some manner with the Sunday school.

1. *The Unsaved Class Members Take Priority*

The teacher should keep in constant contact with the lost members of his class. His visitation will be planned so that they will have priority. He will be alert to every soul-winning opportunity and be prepared to point the way to Christ at any time.

2. *Many Relatives of the Sunday School Members Are Lost*

Multitudes of unsaved parents, brothers, sisters, and others are to be found in the homes of those already enlisted in Sunday school. Many of these can be won to Christ through wise visitation.

3. *The Parents of the Cradle Roll Babies Need to Be Won*

Workers in the Cradle Roll department have a unique opportunity in making possible "A Christian Home for Every Baby." Not only are these workers privileged to visit the unsaved parents, but they may also pray for them and seek to win them to Christ. These workers will find their task a very happy one as they grasp their many soul-winning opportunities

4. *The Members of the Extension Department Must Be Evangelized*

Many lost persons are denied the privilege of hearing the gospel because they cannot attend the church services. The Extension department is ideally suited to search out these neglected ones. Probably no better avenue for visitation-evangelism is available than that which is offered through the Extension department and its work.

5. *The Vacation Bible School Registration Cards Reveal Evangelistic Opportunities*

Multiplied thousands of boys and girls who have no church connection attend Vacation Bible school every year. The homes of these pupils have from one to five adults who are also unsaved. Following up these possibilities is a fruitful field for visitation-evangelism. It offers great enlistment possibilities as well.

II. UNDERSTAND THE REQUIREMENTS FOR VISITATION-EVANGELISM

It is absurd to assume that only the well-instructed may win the lost to Christ. In fact, many less qualified persons put to shame those who know the most about the matter. It is true, however, that to be an effective soul-winner, one needs to have a thorough understanding of the task. There are certain fundamental requirements for visitation-evangelism:

1. *The Visitor Should Know That He Is Genuinely Born Again*

One who cannot swim cannot rescue one who is drowning. He may be the most willing person in the world, but he is not qualified. The person who does not know Christ as his own personal Saviour can hardly tell another how to find Christ.

If there is any doubt about one's own salvation, the matter must certainly be cleared up before attempting to help others. It is easy to know that one is a child of God. The Word says: "But as many as received him, to them gave he power to become the sons of God, even to them that believe on his name" (John 1:12); "That if thou shalt confess with thy mouth the Lord Jesus, and shalt believe in thine heart that God hath raised him from the dead, thou shalt be saved" (Rom. 10:9).

2. *The Visitor Must Understand His Responsibility Toward the Lost*

Christianity is an outgoing religion. To follow Christ in spirit and practice is to feel a deep concern for those who are lost.

(1) *He is commissioned as a soul-winner.*—Every Christian has the explicit command from Christ to go and make disciples. Everything in life must become secondary to this commission to win souls.

(2) *He is charged to be a witness.*—"And ye shall be witnesses unto me" (Acts 1:8). Both by word of mouth and example of life, every born-again soul is obligated and privileged to bear witness to the Saviour. There is no excuse or exemption for any saved person.

(3) *He is entrusted with the gospel.*—"As every man hath received the gift, even so minister the same one to another, as good stewards of the manifold grace of God" (1 Peter 4:10). Every Christian should frequently recall that someone helped him to find Christ. His failure to carry on the work will result in many souls being forever lost. It is indeed a glorious privilege, but it is also a serious responsibility to be entrusted with the gospel of salvation.

(4) *He is responsible to God.*—"I have set thee a watchman ... therefore thou shalt hear the word at my mouth, and warn them from me" (Ezek. 33:7). To be held responsible for the blood of the unsaved is a sobering thought. Escape from such responsibility is gained only through the faithful warning of the wicked by the saved.

Whether or not the unsaved heed the warning is up to them, but the responsibility for warning them is inescapably placed upon every Christian. In the face of this responsibility every Christian will want to be faithful in his task.

3. *The Visitor Must Realize What It Means to Be Lost*

A realization of the condition of a lost soul is the foundation stone of Christian compassion. If there is nothing wrong with an unbeliever, there is no need to seek to help him. It is the realization of the dreadful condition and the ultimate destiny of the lost person that sends the Christian out to help him.

(1) *The lost person is guilty of sin.*—"For all have sinned, and come short of the glory of God" (Rom. 3:23). The unsaved person is guilty of sin before God in a threefold manner: because of disobedience to the will of God; because of an absolute lack of righteousness; and because of a nature that is at enmity with God.

(2) *The lost person is dead in sin.*—Paul states that the lost are "dead in trespasses and sins" (Eph. 2:1). The Old Testament reveals that "the soul that sinneth, it shall die" (Ezek. 18:4), while the New Testament declares, "The wages of sin is death" (Rom. 6:23). It follows that spiritual death, death in trespasses and sin, is the lot of every unbeliever.

(3) *The lost person is condemned before God.*— "He that believeth on him is not condemned: but he that believeth not is condemned already, because he hath not believed in the name of the only begotten Son of God" (John 3:18). The unsaved person will not eventually be condemned; he is already condemned, and the wrath of God abides upon him. This condemnation

places one under the power of Satan, and the Scriptures indict him as a child of Satan: "Ye are of your father the devil" (John 8:44).

(4) *The lost person is without God or hope.*—"That at that time ye were without Christ, . . . having no hope, and without God" (Eph. 2:12). Those who are outside of Christ have no hope either here or hereafter. Imagine the utter hopelessness of having no hope whatever!

(5) *The lost person is facing eternal hell.*—"When the Lord Jesus shall be revealed from heaven with his mighty angels, in flaming fire taking vengeance on them that know not God, and that obey not the gospel of our Lord Jesus Christ: who shall be punished with ever-lasting destruction" (2 Thess. 1:7-9).

4. *The Visitor Must Know the Plan of Salvation*

It would be ridiculous to think that anyone could lead a soul to find Christ if he did not know and thoroughly understand the plan of salvation. The way of salvation is frequently misunderstood. So many human innovations have been added; so many untruthful things have been substituted that the soul-winner should study afresh the old gospel story in all its wonderful simplicity. The plan of salvation is built around the word "all":

(1) All are lost (Rom. 3:23; Isa. 53:6).

(2) All lost persons are condemned (John 3:18; Eph. 2:12).

(3) All lost persons are bound for eternal death (Rom. 6:23; Acts 4:12).

(4) All lost persons may be saved by faith in Christ (Eph. 2:8-9; Acts 3:19; John 3:16; Acts 16:31; John 1:12).

(5) All saved persons should confess Christ (Rom. 10:9-10; Matt. 10:32-33).

5. *The Visitor Should Understand the Problems to Be Solved*

Probably most unsaved persons have some individual difficulty which poses as more or less a real barrier. Exhaustive lists of these problems have been compiled in various books on soul-winning. Every personal worker would do well to secure one of these books and make a study of the various problems to be met. The purpose of this chapter can be served by merely summarizing some of the expected problems. It is quite likely that all of the problems can be listed under the three following heads:

(1) *Genuine misunderstandings.*—Such problems may be readily met with an open Bible. Any person who is willing to be saved can be shown the way. The person who simply does not understand is no real problem to the soul-winner; in fact, this is the easiest of all to reach.

(2) *Prejudiced attitudes.*—This is a difficult type of sinner to reach. The preconceived idea and the prejudiced person will be recognized by statements such as: "I don't like the preacher, choir, teacher, etc."; or perhaps, "I'm just as good as your church members."

Any statement made that is centered in building up the individual reveals an improper attitude. The first thing to remember is not to argue with this person. Admit that none of the church members or preachers, etc., is perfect. Show the individual that God will judge the hypocrite and that he will also judge the unsaved person. Proceed from here with the plan of salvation, praying all the while.

It frequently requires many attempts to win such an individual. In most cases it would be best to try to get the person to attend good, evangelistic, preaching services. When the conviction of the Holy Spirit comes, this person will see himself as a lost sinner, and his prejudice will vanish.

(3) *Hardheartedness.*—The hardhearted person is a baffling problem. In all probability there has been some conviction at one time or another in the heart of this person, and he has refused and hardened his heart. It may have been only a conviction of the conscience and not of the heart.

This type of unsaved person knows what he should do, but he refuses to do it. He will often resent any attempt to help him. He may be rude and gruff. He will seek to make excuses to justify his position. In his resort to alibis he will be likely to state something as follows: "I am doing the best I can, and that is all anyone can do"; "I treat my fellow man right, and if anyone makes it, I will"; "My wife belongs to the _____ church, and I don't want to divide the family."

This individual is not often really sincere, but the wise soul-winner will act as if he believed him to be sincere. The soul-winner will acknowledge that the person is living acceptably in the eyes of the public. He will point out, however, that even though the individual is making an outward success, these things do not go far enough. God demands more. "For the Lord seeth not as man seeth; for man looketh on the outward appearance, but the Lord looketh on the heart" (1 Sam. 16:7). He will proceed by showing the plan of salvation to be one of personal acceptance of Christ rather than a program of self-improvement or personal achievement.

III. FOLLOW THE MASTER'S PROCEDURE IN VISITATION-EVANGELISM

Winning others to Christ in no way depends upon human wisdom and ingenuity, but a practical procedure in dealing with lost people will greatly facilitate the work. It would be impossible to find any better illustration of how to proceed in soul-winning than that in the fourth chapter of John. The master Soul-winner has given a perfect plan for all who would win souls to him. His procedure may be outlined as follows:

1. *Make a Tactful Approach*

The Lord began by making a simple request, "Give me to drink." He thus began at a point of common interest. The woman had come for water, so this need was uppermost in her mind. Nothing else would have interested her so much as water. It is a point worthy of notice that Jesus frequently began his conversations with some object related to life. Talking to someone about his soul is the one thing above all others that is practically related to life.

2. *Create a Deeper Interest*

Jesus appealed to the curiosity of the woman who came for water. He was seeking to deepen her interest more than to hint at her ignorance of his identity when he said, "If thou knewest the gift of God, and who it is that saith to thee, Give me to drink; thou wouldest have asked of him, and he would have given thee living water." Her deep interest was aroused. From this point it was a matter of directing the conversation toward the objective. Awakening a desire for soul-satisfaction depends upon creating a deep interest in one's soul.

3. *Produce a Sense of Conviction*

Jesus tested the effectiveness of his work by saying, "Go, call thy husband, and come hither." Her conscience was smitten, and conviction struck home to her sinful heart as she answered, "I have no husband." Jesus was convinced that she saw herself a lost sinner. He did not berate her; he commended her for telling the truth about not having a husband even though she was trying to cover up her multiplicity of husbands.

4. *Correct a Misunderstanding*

It is a common thing to have an unsaved person bring up some theological problem to sidetrack the discussion. Jesus would not be drawn into controversy about the problem of the place of worship. He quickly dismissed the problem with a brief summary of the truth and left the unsaved woman no opportunity to hide behind a technicality.

Modern-day soul-winners can profit much by this master stroke of Jesus. Not many souls are won to Christ when the soul-winner is led into theological hair splittings. This will frequently destroy the conviction of the Holy Spirit.

5. *Reveal the Way of Salvation*

Jesus hastened to show the woman the way of salvation by revealing himself as the Saviour. The way is so simple and plain that even a child may understand that Jesus alone can forgive sins. Soul-winners must be ever alert that they not make the plan of salvation seem complicated. There are no "ifs," "ands," or "buts." It is simply a matter of a Person.

Salvation is Jesus and Jesus alone, nothing more, nothing less. "Neither is there salvation in any other:

for there is none other name . . . whereby we must be saved" (Acts 4:12). "And this is life eternal, that they might know thee the only true God, and Jesus Christ whom thou hast sent" (John 17:3).

6. *Secure an Open Confession*

Evangelism does not conclude with the salvation of a sinner. The newborn child of God needs to confess Christ. He needs to tell others. He needs the strength that comes from testifying to the saving power of Christ. Jesus did not overlook this matter when dealing with the Samaritan woman, for the Scriptures say, "And many of the Samaritans of that city believed on him for the saying of the woman."

It is a spurious type of evangelism that leaves the new Christian without a profession of his faith before the world. "For with the heart man believeth unto righteousness; and with the mouth confession is made unto salvation" (Rom. 10:10).

7. *Instruct the New Convert*

Not only should the new convert make a profession of his faith, but he should also receive instruction in the Christian life. It is a sin against him to leave him as a helpless babe in Christ. He needs to be given assurance of his salvation. He needs to be led into baptism and church membership. Any personal work that does not include this is falling short of the mark, for saving a soul is not the end; it is just the beginning! Saving the life is equally important.

Every soul-winner should memorize the simple procedure of Jesus in dealing with sinners. It will be found just as effective today as it was in the days of Christ. A little time in learning the procedure will save much time in dealing with individuals and make a more

successful soul-winner. The procedure may be reduced to a mere outline for memorization:

(1) Make a tactful approach.
(2) Create a desire for salvation.
(3) Produce a conviction for sin.
(4) Correct misunderstandings.
(5) Reveal Christ as the way of salvation.
(6) Secure a confession of faith.
(7) Instruct the new convert.

IV. USE THE SCRIPTURES IN VISITATION-EVANGELISM

Every skilful workman must have the proper tools
for his trade. The skilful soul-winner must make use
of his tool, the Word of God. It is the use of the
Scriptures which produces conviction for sin, "For
the word of God is quick, and powerful, and sharper
than any twoedged sword, piercing even to the dividing
asunder of soul and spirit, and of the joints and mar-
row, and is a discerner of the thoughts and intents
of the heart" (Heb. 4:12).

1. *Read the Bible Rather than Quote It*

Regardless of how well the personal worker knows
the Scripture passage to be used, he will be wise to
read the verses rather than quote them. It will be even
more effective to have the unsaved person to do the
reading and then quiz him to see if he understands. It
is this procedure that causes the unsaved person to
see his lost condition as he gazes into the mirror of
God's Word.

2. *Make the Scripture Message Personal*

Another worth-while method of using the Bible is
to reread a passage and substitute the personal pro-

nouns, "I," "me," etc. Instead of "all have come short," use "I have come short of the glory of God," etc. It is also quite effective to use one's own name first and then change it to the sinner's name. There is something about making the Bible very personal that brings swift conviction to a sinful heart.

3. Mark Certain Verses for the Unsaved

One other suggestion for Bible usage is the marking of certain verses in the Bible of the unsaved person. If no Bible is owned by the unsaved person, it would be well for the soul-winner to make a gift of one, at least a Gospel of John. "He that goeth forth and weepeth, bearing precious seed, shall doubtless come again with rejoicing, bringing his sheaves with him" (Psalm 126:6).

FOR CLASS DISCUSSION

Let each member of the study class compile his own list of lost people for whom he is responsible. For this activity members may group themselves according to the age group with which they work. As each group compiles lists of lost relatives of their members, there will (and should) be over-lap in the list. It will be helpful to have the latest available Vacation Bible school enrolment cards on hand. They may reveal evangelistic responsibilities for every department in the Sunday school.

Plan a demonstration of a soul-winning visit. Have one of your number take the role of a lost person. Have another take the role of a soul-winner who uses the Scripture references on pages 92-93.

CHAPTER 9

I. CHEER THE SICK
  1. Understand the Task
  2. Exercise Ordinary Precautions
  3. Use Common Sense
  4. Impart a Spiritual Blessing

II. MINISTER TO THE INCURABLE PATIENT
  1. Guard Against False Reassurances
  2. Hold Out Hope for Eternity

III. COMFORT THE BEREAVED
  1. Make the Call Promptly
  2. Show How to Conquer Grief
  3. Render Practical Service

IV. COUNSEL THE PERPLEXED
  1. Inspire Confidence
  2. Listen Carefully
  3. Seek Solutions Co-operatively

V. ENCOURAGE THE DEJECTED

VI. CULTIVATE HARMONIOUS RELATIONSHIPS
  1. Explain the Church and Its Program
  2. Establish a Warm Fellowship

VII. SECURE CHRISTIAN COMMITMENTS
  1. Lead Others into Definite Service
  2. Promote Stewardship

VIII. STRENGTHEN FAMILY LIFE
  1. Discover Spiritual Problems
  2. Show Parents How to Have Family Worship
  3. Emphasize the Interest of the Church in the Family

Visiting to Render Spiritual Assistance

For I was an hungred, and ye gave me meat: I was thirsty, and ye gave me drink: I was a stranger, and ye took me in: naked, and ye clothed me: I was sick, and ye visited me: I was in prison, and ye came unto me. Matthew 25:35-36

JESUS' ministry was largely characterized by his frequent visits to render spiritual service to those in need. The New Testament gives a large place to the accounts of these services performed by Jesus as well as those of his disciples. No one could question that such a ministry is inherent in the commission, nor that today's task embraces this responsibility.

Times of distress offer the Christian worker, teacher, and pastor an unexcelled opportunity to render spiritual assistance. In some types of visitation one is not always given a situation that has the setting and the opportunity that this ministry offers.

Almost always when one enters a home where sickness and sorrow have come, or where spiritual needs are evident, he will find a warm and sincere welcome. Wherever a need is found, wherever hearts are burdened, wherever emotions are deeply stirred, the "messenger of light" is gratefully received.

I. CHEER THE SICK

One of the most joyful and delightful privileges the Christian has is visiting the sick. Caring for the sick is one of the ministries which Jesus approved when he said: "Inasmuch as ye have done it unto one of the least of these my brethren, ye have done it unto me" (Matt. 25:40).

The sickroom offers an unusually fine opportunity for service. This is true because a person is more responsive during illness than at any other time. There is probably nothing which can discredit a pastor or other worker more quickly than the neglect of the sick. The pastor, Sunday school teacher, or friend should welcome the times when he can minister to the needs of those who are ill. The considerate visitor will:

1. *Understand the Task*

It is of paramount importance that the visitor understand the task of visiting the sick. This type of visitation lies outside the realm of ordinary social contact. The visitor will need to think solely of the person visited. He will bear in mind that a visit can be of utmost significance, either hurtful or helpful.

2. *Exercise Ordinary Precautions*

The visitor will need to give careful thought to the effect of his visit on the sick. There are certain things he will carefully avoid:

(1) *He will not visit the sick without permission from the person on duty whether the visit be in the*

home or in the hospital.—The person on duty bears the responsibility for the patient's well-being.   Therefore, the visitor will respect his wishes and heed his advice.

(2) *He will not enter a sickroom without the patient's being warned.*—A surprise call may be delightful, but it may not be good for the patient. It may prove embarrassing for both the patient and the visitor.   It is always best when visiting in a hospital to have the nurse announce one's presence.   The same is true when visiting in the home.   Some member of the family should announce the visitor to the convalescent.

(3) *He will not make a visit too soon.*—Very few people realize the strain on the patient when he is visited too soon after an operation or severe illness. The patient's vitality is low, and he will not recover as quickly as he ought when his resistance is taxed by too early or too frequent visitation.

(4) *He will not go visiting with a large group.*— Not more than two visitors should ever go into a sickroom.   Too many visitors multiply the drain upon the patient and actually retard the progress of convalescence.

(5) *He will not make the patient uncomfortable.*— It is always best to remain in the direct line of vision so there will be no unnecessary discomfort to the patient.   It is also best to keep a little distance from the bed, especially if the patient has an infectious disease. Touching or sitting on the bed may irritate the patient and often causes pain.   Adjusting the bed or changing the ventilation should be left to the nurse in charge.

(6) *He will not carry strong odors into the room.*— A patient may become annoyed or even nauseated by perfume, tobacco odors, or unusually fragrant flowers. Too many flowers may also disturb the patient.

(7) *He will not take children to see a patient.*—
This practice is not good for either the child or the
patient. Most hospitals prohibit this practice. The
same consideration should be given to those who are
visited in their homes.

(8) *He will not alarm the patient.*—The patient is,
in most cases, anxious about himself and is watching
to see the reactions of the visitors. Regardless of
any anxiety the visitor may feel, he should avoid
expressing it or showing it to the patient.

(9) *He will not take food to the seriously ill.*—
Hospitals have dieticians who work in co-operation
with the doctors to provide the proper food for the
patient. It is presumption to assume that candy or
some other delicacy will be acceptable. It is best to
ask the doctor's permission before bringing any gifts
of food since it is quite possible to cause the patient
undue pain or even complications. Let the specialists
care for the patient's diet.

(10) *He will not stay too long.*—Staying too long
is unforgivable. Under most circumstances from three
to ten minutes will be long enough for anyone to visit
in a sickroom. It is far better for the patient to wish
the visitor would stay longer than to wish that he had
not stayed so long.

3. *Use Common Sense*

Just as there are certain things the wise visitor
will not do in the sickroom, there are other things
which he should do. He will:

(1) *Observe hospital rules and hours.*—The visitor
must realize that the rules and hours of the hospital
are the results of years of experience. They are made
in the best interest of the patient. The visitor who

observes the regulations of the hospital will always
be welcome.

(2) *Speak in a well-modulated voice.*—Speaking too
loudly will disturb not only the one being visited but
also others in the adjoining rooms. On the other hand,
if the visitor whispers, the patient may become apprehensive. In most cases the visitor can avoid the extreme by conversing in a normal voice.

(3) *Display a cheerful attitude.*—It is of inestimable
importance that the visitor create a cheerful attitude.
He should smile, share good news, and seek by every
means to inspirit the patient. Good cheer is not only
helpful, but it is expected by the patient. Its absence
may be a cause for alarm.

4. *Impart a Spiritual Blessing*

A Scripture verse, card, note, poem, or tract may
be left with the patient. This will remind him of the
visit and may frequently be of spiritual help during
his illness.

The visitor should always pray before going to visit
the sick. There might be some occasions, however,
when it would not be best to pray audibly in the sickroom. The patient might assume that the visitor is
unduly alarmed about his condition. On the other
hand, a short prayer may have a very helpful effect on
a patient.

The only certain way to know when prayer is advisable is to ask the leadership of the Holy Spirit.
Prayer should be specific and adapted to the needs of
the individual. It is often the opening for an earnest
conversation about the spiritual needs of the patient.

The visitor should be prepared to read or recite
Scripture passages at the bedside. The passage should

reveal God's care and presence. It should be brief.
Psalm 121; Psalm 107:3; John 14; 1 Peter 5:7; and
Isaiah 12:2; 26:3; 40:11 are good selections for such
occasions. Avoid passages that threaten judgment or
vengance. Use those which lend encouragement, hope,
and comfort.

II. MINISTER TO THE INCURABLE PATIENT

Visiting the patient who is incurable often strikes
terror to the heart of the visitor. It is, however, a
ministry that most Christian workers will be called
upon to render at some time in their experience.

1. *Guard Against False Reassurances*

Usually the patient is aware of his condition before
the visitor arrives. It is not only useless but also
hypocritical for the visitor to offer insincere reassurances. This makes the patient all the more unhappy.
It may even leave him with the feeling that his friends
are not honest enough to face death with him.

2. *Hold Out Hope for Eternity*

It is a blessed privilege to be able to hold out hope
for eternity. In the hour of crisis the visitor may
help patient and family alike to realize that "God is
a very present help in time of trouble." Psalms 91 and
23 are especially appropriate for such occasions.

III. COMFORT THE BEREAVED

On occasions the Christian visitor will have the
privilege of ministering to those who have suffered
the loss of a loved one. Although this is probably
the most difficult service one can render, it is also
probably the most helpful. Standing by in the hour

of bereavement is one of the most appreciated services
that pastors and Sunday school workers can render.

1. *Make the Call Promptly*

The visit should be made to the home of the bereaved as soon as possible. Under the stress of deep
emotion the bereaved expect an immediate visit from
the pastor and friends. Much of the good that can be
accomplished is lost after a few hours have passed.
Regardless of inconveniences it is essential that the
visit be made at once.

2. *Show How to Conquer Grief*

After speaking a few words of sympathy the visitor
should read from the Bible and pray with those who are
bereaved. He may help the family overcome their grief
by suggesting the following thoughts:

(1) Remember the happy estate of a departed Christian.

(2) Remember the prospect of an eventual reunion.

(3) Remember the constant presence of Christ.

One need not be overly concerned about what to say.
The fact that an interest is shown will be sufficient
to warrant the visit.

3. *Render Practical Service*

There will be many arrangements and details needing
attention in the time of grief. The Christian friend
has a marvelous opportunity for showing the practical
side of Christianity. He can give help by contacting
relatives, providing meals, helping with transportation
to the funeral home, and by attending to many other
details essential to such an experience.

Above all, it must be remembered that the lonely days following the funeral need to be filled with companionship. The pastor and other visitors will need to call again soon after the interment to lend every assistance in the days of adjustment.

IV. COUNSEL THE PERPLEXED

There are many occasions for counseling those who need spiritual assistance. It will be wise, of course, to leave the serious problems to those who are trained and qualified for the task. However, there are many ways in which a Christian visitor may render great help to those who are facing spiritual problems.

There are three definite steps in helping those who have such problems:

1. *Inspire Confidence*

It will be impossible to be of any specific help until the counselee feels free to tell what he has on his heart. There must be an air of confidence, freedom, and relaxation. A kind and sympathetic attitude in conversation is the key.

2. *Listen Carefully*

Most people are eager to talk and to tell their burdens. They want to confide in someone who understands. Actually most of the problem is solved by the simple expedient of sharing it with a sympathetic listener.

Many persons who have no disturbing problems long for fellowship with some kindly visitor. In cases of this type, conversation becomes an actual process in counseling, even though there is no problem to be solved or help to be offered.

3. *Seek Solutions Co-operatively*

Simply talking it over will not always be sufficient help for those in spiritual distress. Often a more direct approach will be necessary.

(1) *Discover the source of trouble.*—Not only must the problem be honestly faced, but the underlying cause must be ferreted out. Frequently a misunderstanding, an improper attitude, or even a slight may create a real problem. Personal differences, personal clashes, or disagreements can cause serious spiritual problems. Regardless of the source of trouble, it must be brought into the open before progress can be made.

(2) *Find possible solutions.*—Probably the most effective way to do this will be to write down all of the possibilities as they come to mind. This will aid in an unemotional consideration of the various approaches. It will also facilitate making a disposition of the problem in an objective manner. Whenever possible a parallel situation in the Bible should be used as a guide. Perhaps the visitor has had a similar experience which will furnish a helpful pattern.

(3) *Make the proper choice.*—The visitor, while counseling, will merely guide toward a solution. The choice must always be made by the person having the problem. The visitor will, of course, lead as far as possible toward a scriptural, Christian way of solving every problem.

V. ENCOURAGE THE DEJECTED

Someone has said that the most priceless gift anyone can give is encouragement. This is particularly true in the spiritual realm. Most people are plagued with discouragement at one time or another.

Sunday school pupils need encouragement. Many of the pupils are not mature Christians. They need to be encouraged and strengthened in their Christian experience. Those who are discouraged will appreciate a visit from a sympathetic, understanding teacher.

Sunday school teachers and officers frequently need encouragement. Probably discouragement is the main reason for the great turnover in volunteer church personnel. Discerning pastors and Sunday school superintendents will be able to save many potentially strong workers by lending appropriate words of encouragement at the right time.

Every church has some "forgotten members"—the older members, those whose physical condition keeps them away, those whose employment causes frequent absence. All of these need encouragement and consolation.

Those who visit for the Extension department of the Sunday school are especially privileged to minister to persons who miss the encouragement and fellowship of the services.

VI. CULTIVATE HARMONIOUS RELATIONSHIPS

The visitor who is sensitive to the needs of those he is visiting will soon discover that there are manifold opportunities to cultivate harmonious relationships. He will accept these as occasions to interpret any unsatisfactory conditions.

1. *Explain the Church and Its Program*

New Christians will need help in understanding and appreciating their new church home. Something of its history, background, and beliefs should be given them.

Its relation to other churches and the denomination should also be explained.

2. *Establish a Warm Fellowship*

Improving the fellowship is one of the most important aspects of visitation. Every church will have some few members who do not like the Sunday school class, the choir, the pastor, or some phase of the program. Visitors who seek to pour oil on troubled waters are God's choice servants. Those who seek to salvage one who wanders from the truth render a signal service. "If any one among you wanders from the truth and some one brings him back, let him know that whoever brings back a sinner from the error of his way will save his soul from death and will cover a multitude of sins" (James 5:19 RSV).

VII. SECURE CHRISTIAN COMMITMENTS

The Lord uses human instrumentality to lay his claims upon the hearts of his people. The best results are accomplished when this is done by personal contact. The Christian visitor will be called upon to:

1. *Lead Others into Definite Service*

Jesus always sought his workers personally. He did not resort to volunteers; rather he sought out the person best endowed to do the task. One of the greatest privileges a visitor can have is to lay the challenge of a Christian task on the heart of another and help him choose to do it.

2. *Promote Stewardship*

It is an annual occurrence in many churches to conduct an every-member canvass. The success of this campaign depends largely upon competent visitors.

VIII. Strengthen Family Life

The need for a ministry to family life is evidenced on every hand by the general instability of many homes. Perhaps no type of visitation embodies such possibilities for service as visitation to render a spiritual ministry to a family. Practically every visitor has the opportunity to undergird and strengthen family life. Many areas of need will be discerned by the thoughtful visitor. The following fields are only suggestive:

1. *Discover Spiritual Problems*

As the Christian visitor wins the confidence of a home, he can, through observation and tactful conversation, discover its spiritual problems. Perhaps the visitor has experienced or observed a similar problem and can share the way in which the solution was reached. Certainly the visitor will offer the wisdom of God's Word. Many times *Home Life* magazine can be helpful as it shows how other families have solved such problems as broken homes, non-Christian homes, unsaved and indifferent parents or children, mixed faiths, and maladjustment of family members to each other.

2. *Show Parents How to Have Family Worship*

Family worship in the home is as old as the historical and biblical recordings of the home. Actually family worship is the richest heritage parents can leave their children. Yet many homes have never experienced the blessing of sacred moments spent daily in family Bible reading and prayer.

The visitor in the home without family worship will want to show the family the why and how of conducting such a period. He should be able to suggest the best time to have it, how to use the Scriptures, how to secure every member participation. He will find *Home*

Life magazine an invaluable aid and a most welcome gift as he shows the family how to accomplish a satisfying worship experience.

3. *Emphasize the Interest of the Church in the Family*

Some parents would be surprised to know that the church has an interest in the spiritual welfare of the home. The visitor should help them to see that the church and the home are decreed by God to be allies in society, and that the welding of these two units into a spiritual co-operative is a primary concern of the church. Parents should be led to see that a partial estimate of the interest of the church in the home is demonstrated by the provision of a Christian family magazine, *Home Life,* for its members.

It is, of course, impossible to list all of the ways in which a Christian who really loves the Lord may render service. However, in the ministry of visitation he most nearly approaches the exact work and method employed by Christ himself. It is in personal visitation that the Christian finds himself, loses himself, and gives himself in the most unselfish way to doing the will of God. Surely to the faithful visitor the Lord will say, "Well done, thou good and faithful servant" (Matt. 25:21).

FOR CLASS DISCUSSION

Share with one another some testimonies of experiences in visiting to meet some of the spiritual needs discussed in this chapter.

SUGGESTIONS FOR THE TEACHER

Who Will Lead In The Study of This Book

Study the author's foreword. Think of the visitation program in the church, or churches, to be represented in the class that will meet with you for a study of this book. What actual changes in the visitation program are needed?

Study the table of contents. Chapter 1 gives motivation for this study. Chapters 2, 3, and 6 deal with the program to be realized by the church as a whole under the direction of the pastor and key leaders. Chapters 4, 5, 8, and 9 deal with qualities and skills to be developed by the individual Christian. Chapter 7 motivates a teacher's visitation (and to a large extent visitation by class members).

PURPOSE

The consideration suggested in the foregoing paragraphs will help you to formulate a general statement of purpose prior to the first class period. As members register for the class during the first period, ask each to indicate what he hopes to get out of this study. Later, seek to analyze the replies in order to determine the needs of which your class members are aware. If the replies are meager or not very specific, you will recognize that one of your teaching aims will be to lead class members to feel a definite sense of need.

LEARNING ACTIVITIES

Much of the study of this book should be of the project, or clinic, type. The discussions in class periods should be for the purpose of motivating, guiding, and evaluating actual efforts to practice the suggestions in this book. Visitation assignments should be made to class members and be carried out during the week of study.

Chapter 1 may be developed from the chapter outline (on the chalkboard on a previously prepared chart). The development should include Scripture searching and reading by class members to authenticate the author's statements.

Chapters 2 and 3 may be a problem-solving project: How shall we proceed in our church to develop and maintain an effective program of visitation?

Ask the class to consider the suggestions set forth in the chapter outlines. Ask each individual mentally to compare what his church is now doing with what the author proposes, and to mention changes in his church plan which will be needed if the author's suggestions are followed.

As a summary, you may use the motion picture *Sent Forth* (16 min.) or the filmstrip *Bring Them In* (35 frames selected from the motion picture).

Chapter 4 should be a heart-searching study. Each member may use the chapter outline (page 40) as a self-rating chart and check himself *good, average,* or *poor* on each point suggested.

The motion picture *He That Winneth* (15 min.) or the corresponding filmstrip *He That Reapeth* (36 frames) relate closely to chapter 4.

Chapter 5 will have a two-fold relationship to the visitation being done as clinical work in connection with the study of this book. (1) As members report visits made to date during the course of this study, lead the class to evaluate the techniques in the light of their previous (home) study of chapter 5. Seek to determine how these visits could have been made more effective. (2) Use the chapter for guidance as class members make plans to visit individuals whose names have been assigned (either previously or during the class period).

There is good opportunity for role playing as one class member takes the part of a visitor and another assumes the role of a prospect who should be led to attend Sunday school. Follow the role playing by a period of evaluation, applying the questions on page 62.

Instead of role playing by class members, the motion picture *How To Visit* may be studied by the class and evaluated according to the questions on page 62.

Chapter 6 can be approached as a planning activity based on the problem: How can our church secure more significant results in Sunday school enlargement through an improved visitation program?

The motion picture *And Make Disciples* (15 min.) or the filmstrip *Ye Are Witnesses* (36 frames) may be used, if time permits.

Chapter 7 may be developed in class as the members compile their own lists of reasons why a teacher needs to visit. Then lead them to examine the author's outline for any reasons they may have failed to include in their lists.

Chapters 8 and 9 lend themselves to activities similar to those suggested for chapter 5.

In connection with these chapters you may wish to use the motion picture *Sword of the Spirit* (13 min.) or selected frames from this picture in the filmstrip *Words of Life* (36 frames).

FOR REVIEW AND WRITTEN WORK

CHAPTER I

1. What plan did Jesus give for carrying on his work?
2. Name some of the ways in which Jesus visited.
3. Explain briefly what part visitation played in the life of the New Testament churches.
4. What evidence do we have that visitation helped in the early spread of Christianity?

CHAPTER II

1. Name the six steps in developing a systematic program of visitation.
2. What kind of person should be chosen for the superintendent of enlargement?
3. List some of the best ways of finding Sunday school prospects.
4. What are the advantages of a concerted visitation program?

CHAPTER III

1. Why should the visitation program be permanent?
2. Suggest ways in which the visitation program may be kept before the people.
3. What method may be used to guarantee that all absentees, prospects, and members will be visited regularly?
4. List some ways in which visitors may be trained.

CHAPTER IV

1. After an honest evaluation of your present attitude toward visitation, how do you plan to make improvements?
2. Discuss briefly the personality traits which a conscientious visitor should seek to develop.
3. What personal preparation should the visitor make?
4. Suggest the spiritual preparation which should be made before visiting.

CHAPTER V

1. What are some of the steps in mastering the art of visitation?
2. What do you consider an impressive contact?
3. How does the skilful visitor guide the conversation?
4. How may a visitor guarantee that his work will be effective and profitable?

CHAPTER VI

1. Explain briefly how a desire for Sunday school enlargement can be developed.
2. List the duties of the class officers in visitation.
3. How does the department organization aid in effective visitation?
4. Discuss briefly the ways in which it is possible to reach the last person.

CHAPTER VII

1. In what ways does visitation help the teacher understand the pupil?

2. Name the ways in which visitation helps the teacher plan his lesson procedure.
3. Show how visitation helps the teacher make his teaching practical.
4. How do visitation and frequent association with the pupil help the teacher test his teaching?

CHAPTER VIII

1. Mention some opportunities for visitation-evangelism.
2. What do you consider to be the chief characteristics of one who visits to win the lost?
3. List the steps that Jesus used in visitation-evangelism.
4. Discuss briefly how the Scripture passages can be used in winning the lost.

CHAPTER IX

1. Name some ordinary precautions to be observed when visiting the sick.
2. Explain briefly several ways of imparting a spiritual blessing to those who are ill.
3. Name three definite steps in counseling the perplexed.
4. Give examples of Christian commitments which the visitor may have a chance to secure.